The Best

ROTISSERIE CHICKEN COOKBOOK

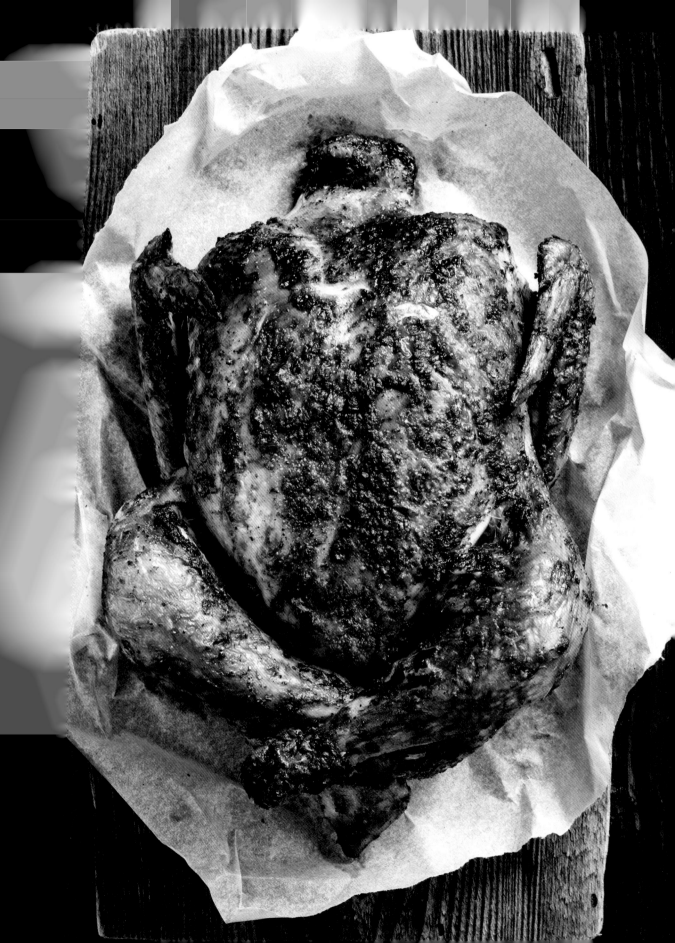

The Best

ROTISSERIE CHICKEN COOKBOOK

100 TASTY RECIPES USING A STORE-BOUGHT BIRD

TOBY AMIDOR

Robert ROSE

DISCLAIMER
The recipes in this book have been carefully tested by our kitchen and our tasters. To the best of our knowledge, they are safe and nutritious for ordinary use and users. For those people with food or other allergies, or who have special food requirements or health issues, please read the suggested contents of each recipe carefully and determine whether or not they may create a problem for you. All recipes are used at the risk of the consumer.

We cannot be responsible for any hazards, loss or damage that may occur as a result of any recipe use.

For those with special needs, allergies, requirements or health problems, in the event of any doubt, please contact your medical adviser prior to the use of any recipe.

At the time of publication, all URLs referenced link to existing websites. Robert Rose Inc. is not responsible for maintaining, and does not endorse the content of, any website or content not created by Robert Rose Inc.

DESIGN AND PRODUCTION: Kevin Cockburn/PageWave Graphics Inc.
EDITOR: Kate Bolen
PROOFREADER: Karen Levy
INDEXER: Ken DellaPenta

COVER IMAGE: © gettyimages.com/mphillips007 (chicken); © gettyimages.com/Arthit_Longwilai (background); © gettyimages.com/Serhii Sereda (knife and fork icon)
INTERIOR PHOTOGRAPHY: © gettyimages.com/Warren_Price (page 1); © gettyimages.com/ivandzyuba (page 2); © gettyimages.com/LightFieldStudios (page 5); © gettyimages.com/BigNazik (pages 6-7); © gettyimages.com/John Foxx (page 10); © gettyimages.com/AtnoYdur (page 12); © gettyimages.com/Art_rich (page 13); © gettyimages.com/rez-art (page 18); © gettyimages.com/Easy_Asa (page 20); © gettyimages.com/Julia_Sudnitskaya (page 32); © gettyimages.com/ Zenobillis (page 34); © gettyimages.com/Brycia James (page 38); © gettyimages.com/RondaKimbrow (page 44); © gettyimages.com/hongquang09 (page 49); © gettyimages.com/derketta (page 52); © gettyimages.com/barol16 (page 56); © gettyimages.com/mphillips007 (page 59); © gettyimages.com/Björn Forenius (page 62); © gettyimages.com/ kasia2003 (page 67); © gettyimages.com/Magone (page 74); © gettyimages.com/klenova (page 80); © gettyimages.com/ bgsmith (page 85); © gettyimages.com/AnnaPustynnikova (page 88); © shutterstock.com/Liudmyla Chuhunova (page 94); © gettyimages.com/DreamBigPhotos (page 99); © gettyimages.com/yodaswaj (page 103); © gettyimages.com/Bartosz Luczak (page 107); © gettyimages.com/AlexPro9500 (page 111); © gettyimages.com/crispphotography (page 117); © gettyimages.com/Floortje (page 121); © gettyimages.com/vm2002 (page 123); © gettyimages.com/ilzesgimene (page 124); © gettyimages.com/DebbiSmirnoff (page 131); © gettyimages.com/OlgaMiltsova (page 141); © gettyimages.com/ LauriPatterson (page 156); © gettyimages.com/Brycia James (page 159); © gettyimages.com/ivi (page 162); © gettyimages.com/VeselovaElena (page 168); © gettyimages.com/asab974 (page 173); © gettyimages.com/spafra (page 175); © gettyimages.com/fatihhoca (page 184); © gettyimages.com/Arthit_Longwilai (chapter opener backgrounds)

Published by Robert Rose Inc.
120 Eglinton Avenue East, Suite 800, Toronto, Ontario, Canada M4P 1E2
Tel: (416) 322-6552 Fax: (416) 322-6936
www.robertrose.ca

Printed and bound in Canada

1 2 3 4 5 6 7 8 9 DPSG 27 26 25 24 23 22 21 20

To my favorite three taste testers,
Schoen, Ellena and Micah — I love you very much.
Always remember three magical words:
Mom's always right.

CONTENTS

INTRODUCTION

AS A SINGLE working mother of three kids in their teens and tweens, I constantly juggle family, work and me time. However, as a registered dietitian (RD) and mom, I am frequently torn between finding time to cook healthy meals for my family and giving in to buying ready-made meals that may have less than healthful ingredients. You would think that over the years — through cooking regularly for my family, working as the nutrition expert for FoodNetwork.com, developing recipes for renowned chefs and writing several cookbooks — I would have mastered all of the tricks for quickly preparing a meal. It's true that I've learned so many quick and easy ways to prepare delicious dishes, but sometimes that's just not enough. I still need to find shortcuts to get nourishing meals on the table. Enter the exceptionally convenient rotisserie chicken.

The first time I brought home a rotisserie chicken, it was to test a recipe for a cookbook I was working on. I had pulled off the chicken from the bones, put it in a bowl and stepped out of the kitchen for a moment. Upon my return I discovered that someone had eaten almost the entire bowl of chicken: my youngest daughter! I had to run to the store and bought two more rotisserie chickens, one for my recipe and one for my daughter, who was happy to eat rotisserie chicken over the next few days.

Ever since then, I have added rotisserie chicken in my healthy meal repertoire. My youngest still enjoys her rotisserie chicken right off the bone and dipped in ketchup or barbecue sauce, but we have also evolved the way we eat these tasty, convenient birds to include quesadillas, tacos, grilled cheese, over salads and as chicken salad.

HOW TO USE THIS BOOK

In chapter 1 I explain the terms you may see on your bird so you can make the best decision for you and your family. If you've ever purchased a rotisserie chicken, you may have noticed there are various types of chickens available, including those labeled as "natural" or "organic." You possibly also noticed that rotisserie chickens are often smaller than an average whole, raw chicken, or you may have questioned how they are raised. And let's not forget about concerns of antibiotic and hormone usage. All of these labels and considerations can get confusing. There is no right or wrong answer to what you choose — it is simply a personal choice.

Everyone has their own cooking preferences and needs. Some people cook for themselves, others cook for two, and of course, you may be cooking for an entire family. In chapter 2, I provide tips, tricks and do's and don'ts for each of these lifestyles, along with meal ideas. If you like to cook recipes with five ingredients or less, put dinner on the table in 15 minutes or less or want to meal prep for the week ahead, I provide guidance and a recipe list for each.

One of the key benefits of buying a rotisserie chicken is how quickly you can get a meal on the table. But let me tell you that after a while, eating chicken off the bone can get a little boring. This cookbook helps you take rotisserie chicken to the next level with new and enticing ways to serve it. You'll find recipes for breakfast, appetizers and snacks, soups and sandwiches, salads and main dishes. It's so easy to incorporate rotisserie chicken in favorites like lasagna, burgers, grilled cheese and pasta dishes. You'll also find a handful of simple grain and vegetable side dishes you can prepare regularly to go with many dishes, as well as dressings, sauces and condiments you can use for salads, main dishes or dipping those freshly carved pieces of chicken.

My "Toby's Tips" are provided at the end of every recipe. There you'll find recommendations for ways to lighten up a recipe, what to serve with the dish or suggestions to modify the flavor to your liking. Many of the recipes in this book share an added benefit or feature. Keep an eye out for the following icons:

| 5 Ingredients or Less | 15 minutes or Less | Freezer-Friendly | Meal Prep | One Pot or Pan |

Take the time to try a variety of recipes and see which ones meet the flavor palate of you and your family. I am quite certain that you will find many dishes that will make a regular appearance in your weekly meal rotation. So get your pots and pans ready to take an adventure into the versatility of rotisserie chicken. Let me tell you, you'll be amazed at how quick and easy the recipes are!

CHAPTER 1
ROTISSERIE 101

IT'S NO WONDER that the rotisserie chicken has become a staple of weeknight dinners. Folks are looking to simplify dinnertime during the hectic workweek, and what could be more convenient than a delicious, hot, ready-to-eat chicken that was flavored and cooked on rotating spits? With a precooked bird, there's no need to handle raw chicken or worry about disinfecting your counter, and you can shave at least 15 minutes off your weeknight dinner routine.

The introduction of rotisserie chicken began in 1985, when fast casual restaurant chain Boston Market, originally called Boston Chicken, specialized in the sale of these birds. The concept of bringing home a ready-to-eat chicken, served along with several side dishes, for a prep-free family dinner that felt home cooked was embraced by the public. Eventually the company expanded its offerings to turkey, meatloaf, ribs and ham and changed its name to Boston Market.

Over the years, more and more people began looking to pick up prepared foods for quick and easy dinners — and supermarkets and club member stores responded by providing this value-added service. Walk into any grocery store and you will find premade sandwiches, salads, hot meals and prepared dishes to heat and eat. Rotisserie chicken fits this convenience trend, and sales of rotisserie chicken are unbelievably high. According to the National Chicken Council, rotisserie chicken sales in 2018 were close to nine hundred million, with about seven hundred million of those birds expected to be bought at the retail level (grocery stores and club member stores). In turn, rotisserie chicken has become a household phenomenon.

Rotisserie chickens can now be found in all sorts of markets, from traditional grocery stores to healthy food stores like Whole Foods to club member stores like Costco. Although most stores purchase the birds from distributors, Costco decided to take full control of the entire process — from farm to customer. Customers increasingly want to know where their food comes from, and controlling the flow of food from the farm through customer sales is a trend retailers are adopting. For example, both Walmart and Kroger supply some or all of the milk they sell in their stores. In addition to the farm to table trend, many poultry companies are now raising larger birds for their parts, which then get processed as nuggets and other dishes, as opposed to the smaller birds required for rotisserie. With Costco reportedly selling about sixty million rotisserie chickens every year (in 2017, they sold eighty-seven million!), maintaining control of their supply chain makes sense for the company.[1] Barns in Nebraska and Iowa are estimated to

[1] Grant Gerlock, "Costco Becomes First Retailer to Control Its Entire Chicken Supply Chain," *Harvest Public Media*, October 23, 2018, https://www.harvestpublicmedia.org/post/costco-becomes-first-retailer-control-its-entire-chicken-supply-chain.

supply about 40 percent of the rotisserie chicken and chicken parts Costco needs. According to a report from the Knowledge Exchange research program at the farming bank CoBank, rotisserie sales at Costco have grown by more than 8 percent per year since 2010,[2] and they reportedly now sell an average of 157,000 chickens a day.[3]

[2] "Costco Poultry Complex Could Redefine Farm-to-Fork," CoBank, September 20, 2018, https://www1.cobank.com/corporate/news/costco-poultry-complex-could-redefine-farm-to-fork.
[3] Juliana LaBianca, "There's an Unsettling Reason Why Your Costco Rotisserie Chicken Tastes So Good," *Business Insider*, February 6, 2018, https://www.businessinsider.com/theres-a-secret-ingredient-in-costcos-famous-rotisserie-chicken-2018-2.

WHY PICK UP A ROTISSERIE CHICKEN?

There are many advantages to picking up a rotisserie chicken on your way home from work — or to stock up for the week ahead. So the next time you're at your local grocery store, here are five reasons to consider picking up one or two.

1. **It's budget friendly.** Rotisserie chickens are sold at reasonable prices ranging from around $3.99 to $9.99 U.S. dollars per bird. According to statistics portal Statista, Americans spent over $7,000 a year on food in 2016, which increased in subsequent years. In 2016, most folks in the U.S. purchased groceries at supermarkets or supercenter stores like Walmart and made between one and three shopping trips per week.[4] With many folks making multiple trips to the store weekly and trying to cut back on grocery bills, it's easy to see the appeal of an inexpensive ready-to-eat bird.

2. **It saves time.** Say goodbye to long prep times, especially during your busy workweek. When using a rotisserie chicken, you don't have to separate the raw foods from the ready-to-eat foods or handle raw chicken and worry about salmonella being spread throughout the kitchen. You don't have to remember to thaw the chicken (how many times have you forgotten?!) or worry about how long it will take the meal to cook up. By using a rotisserie chicken you can save a *minimum* of 15 minutes for recipes and up to several hours, depending on the recipe.

3. **It's versatile.** Rotisserie chicken is delicious on its own, but more importantly, it can be used in a wide variety of dishes, like the recipes you'll find in this cookbook. There are eighty-nine recipes using rotisserie chicken, with twenty recipes for easy sides, condiments, sauces and dips to go with your bird. Recipes you will find in this cookbook include breakfast dishes like Chicken and Vegetable Breakfast Frittata (page 37), appetizers like Chicken Stuffed Baked Potato Skins (page 48), snacks like Chicken Avocado Toast (page 51), soups like Hearty Root Vegetable and Chicken Soup (page 63), sandwiches like Chicken Club Wrap (page 76), salads like Buffalo Chicken Salad (page 83) and main dishes like White Bean and Chicken Chili (page 130) and Chicken Pot Pie (page 120).

4. **It's a recipe shortcut.** Using a rotisserie chicken in recipes helps circumvent more complicated steps in recipes. For example, when making chicken lasagna you would need to prepare your raw meat mixture and then make sure that it is cooked through before assembling the rest of the dish. Skipping that step and using a rotisserie chicken in Chicken and Cheese Lasagna (page 104) helps not only save time but also simplifies the recipe so it is easier to make. The same is true for Sweet Potato Chicken Chili (page 109), Chicken Pot Pie (page 120) and nearly all of the recipes in this book.

5. **It's easy and nutritious.** The tradeoff for so many convenience foods is that if it's easy and affordable, it may not be good for you. Rotisserie chicken provides a variety of nutrients to keep your body healthy. These nutrients include protein and a variety of vitamins and minerals, including riboflavin, niacin, vitamin B_6, pantothenic acid, phosphorus, zinc and selenium. A deeper look at the nutrition of rotisserie chicken can be found on page 19.

---

[4] Emma Bedford, "U.S. Food Shopping Behavior - Statistics & Facts," Statista, October 30, 2018, https://www.statista.com/topics/1527/food-shopping-behavior.

WHERE ARE ROTISSERIE CHICKENS SOURCED AND RAISED?

Chickens that are raised for meat are called "broilers," while birds that are raised for their eggs are called "layers." Confusingly, "broiler" is also the name of the smallest size and weight category of, you guessed it, broilers. If you think rotisserie chickens appear smaller than your typical 4 pound (2 kg) whole chicken, you may be right. Why are they smaller? Smaller chickens are younger compared to larger ones and they go by different names. Here is a rundown of the names and sizes of chicken you can find at the store:

BROILER AGE AND WEIGHT CATEGORIES

NAME OF CHICKEN	AGE	WEIGHT
Broilers	6 to 8 weeks old	2½ lbs (1.25 kg)
Fryers	6 to 8 weeks old	2½ to 3½ lbs (1.25 to 1.75 kg)
Roasters	Less than 8 months old	3½ to 5 lbs (1.75 to 2.5 kg)
Stewing chickens	Over 10 months old (usually hens)	5 to 7 lbs (2.5 to 3.5 kg)
Capons	Castrated male chickens	6 to 8 lbs (3 to 4 kg)
Cocks (or roosters)	Male chickens over 10 months old	6 to 8 lbs (3 to 4 kg)

Rotisserie chicken are made from smaller chickens and cooked whole. Larger chickens tend to be used for their parts (like wings or breasts).

So how does the process begin? Initially, chicken companies purchase one-day-old pullets, which are breeder chicks. At twenty weeks the pullets join the hens and roosters on the farm so they can produce fertilized eggs (not table eggs). The eggs are collected and delivered to hatcheries, where they are incubated and hatched into chickens that are used for meat. Those chicks are transported from the hatchery to local family farms, where they live in barns that are equipped with advanced heating and ventilation systems. The chicks are raised in large, open structures called houses, where they can roam, eat and socialize with other chicken and have access to a veterinarian. About twenty-five thousand chickens live together in each house. Broiler chickens take about seven weeks to grow to the weight the market requires, and once the chickens reach the desired age and size, they all leave together for processing in plants that must adhere to strict government guidelines.

HOW ARE ROTISSERIE CHICKENS PREPARED?

Once the chickens are processed, they are brought to another facility to be flavored according to the specifications of the purchasing grocery, before being shipping to the store. Some stores offer rotisserie chickens either with or without seasoning. A seasoned bird is typically injected with a special saline solution, which adds both flavor and salt, and will be included on the ingredients list. The nutrition facts panel on the package lists all of the ingredients added to the bird, so you can decide which rotisserie chicken is right for you and your family. When using a rotisserie chicken for a recipe, opt for regular (or unflavored) rotisserie chicken since you will be flavoring it. Select a chicken that is plump and appears to have more meat on the bone.

At the grocery the chickens are skewered on spits (a long solid rod) and placed in a rotisserie oven to slowly rotate and fully cook until the skin is golden and crisp. Each rotisserie oven has numerous spits, so stores are able to cook quite a few at a time. Markets will cook rotisserie chickens in the morning, often around 10:00 or 11:00 a.m., and place the cooked chickens on a heated shelf to keep them warm. You can always ask your local store what time they cook their rotisserie chickens so that you can get there right after they are made. Some stores offer cooled cooked chickens, which are kept in refrigerated grab and go displays. It's possible your local store also provides the option of rotisserie chicken meat off the bone so you have even less work to do at home, but this isn't permitted in all areas.

FOOD SAFETY AND STORAGE

According to food safety guidelines, rotisserie chickens must be held at or above 135°F (58°C) and can be held throughout the day at this temperature (as long as they don't go below it for a prolonged period of time). Once you've selected your fully cooked rotisserie chicken, you want it to be hot at the time of purchase (except refrigerated rotisserie, which should be cold). You should be able to feel the heat radiating from the surface of the rotisserie chicken case, and the container should be pretty hot. When shopping, I recommend picking up the rotisserie chicken last, right before checkout. That way it spends as little time as possible at room temperature. You also want to bring your rotisserie chicken straight home and not leave it in a hot car — that is a food safety no-no.

When you get a bird home from the store, make sure that it is fully cooked. According to food safety standards, the internal temperature of a fully cooked chicken reached at least 165°F (75°C). If you find that the white meat of the chicken appears pinkish, or if you just have a "bad feeling," then return it to the store. As the saying goes, "when in doubt, toss it out." Fortunately, in this case, you can return it. Also be on the lookout for overcooked rotisserie chicken, which may have a green or gray tinge to the meat. Overcooked chicken isn't tasty and should also be returned to the store.

Use your rotisserie chicken within two hours or remove the meat, place in a shallow container, cover and refrigerate. Refrigerated rotisserie chicken should be eaten within three to four days, either cold or reheated to 165°F (75°C). You can also freeze rotisserie chicken. For the best quality, flavor and texture, use frozen rotisserie chicken within four months. Dishes made from rotisserie chicken and then frozen should be used within two months.

FREE-RANGE, CAGE-FREE AND OTHER TERMS

There are many different terms used to describe how a rotisserie chicken was raised. Most broiler chickens in the U.S. are grown in enclosed barns in order to keep them safe from predators, extreme weather conditions, insects and possible introduction of diseases, like bird flu. Chickens also feel a sense of security when they are together in an enclosed house. Access to the outdoors varies, depending on the farmers' preferences. "Free-range" chickens have some access to go outside (whether they go outside or not is up to them). According to the National Chicken Council, there's no federal government definition of "free-range," so the U.S. Department of Agriculture (USDA) approves these label claims on a case-by-case basis.[5] It should be noted that all organic chickens must also be free-range; however, not all free-range chickens are organic. At most farms, free-range chickens are brought inside at night in order to protect them from predators, like coyotes. You may have also seen labels that say "cage-free" chicken. However, broilers are not caged and they are free to roam around in their large open houses.

In addition to "free-range" and "cage-free," there are a number of other labels that you may see. Here is a rundown of what they each mean.

ALL-VEGETABLE OR VEGETARIAN DIET: Poultry feed is usually made from corn and soybean meal. On occasion they may also contain meat and poultry by-products, which provide an array of vitamins, minerals and protein. If the feed does not contain any of these meat or poultry ingredients, it can be labeled as "All-Vegetable Diet" or "Veggie Fed."

FARM-RAISED: In the U.S. all chickens raised for meat are farm-raised in spacious barns or houses with technologically advanced ventilation systems and temperature controls. They also have clean feeding and water systems.

NATURAL: According to the U.S. Department of Agriculture, a chicken labeled as "natural" has no artificial ingredients, coloring ingredients or chemical preservatives.

---

5 "Chickopedia: What Consumers Need to Know," National Chicken Council, accessed November 12, 2019, https://www.nationalchickencouncil.org/about-the-industry/chickopedia.

ORGANIC: The "USDA Certified Organic" seal is regulated by the U.S. Department of Agriculture. The seal means that the chicken has been fed only certified organic feed, made with corn and soybeans. The chicken also must be free-range (have outdoor access) and not been given antibiotics. Organic chicken may have been vaccinated against common diseases. It should be noted that the organic label does not mean that the safety, quality or nutrient composition is better or higher than conventionally raised chicken.

NO ADDED HORMONES OR STEROIDS: Although food may be labeled as "no added hormones" or "no added steroids," chickens raised in the U.S. are not given added hormones or steroids. Using natural or artificial hormones on chickens raised for food is not allowed by the Food and Drug Administration.

ENHANCED: A prepared chicken is "enhanced" if it has marinade or ingredients added for flavor, such as water, salt, sugar, chicken broth or seasonings (like garlic). If a chicken is enhanced it must be clearly labeled as such on the front of the package. The label must also list all the ingredients and how much was used.

WHAT ABOUT ANTIBIOTICS?

Farmers are continuously trying to find new innovations to allow chickens to be raised without the use of antibiotics. The use of antibiotics is strictly regulated by the U.S. Food and Drug Administration (FDA) and used as a tool to keep chickens healthy. Other tools that are used to keep a bird healthy include individualized nutrition plans (animal nutritionists do exist!), the use of vaccines and probiotics, barns with good air circulation and temperature control, and training and education programs for farmers and farmworkers.

However, chickens do become ill for various reasons and treating sick animals is part of humane animal care. Antibiotics are determined to be necessary after the animal is seen by animal health experts and veterinarians. If a chicken is given antibiotics within its life to treat or prevent disease, the bird must go through withdrawal before leaving the farm in order to allow the antibiotics to pass through its system. Both the FDA and the USDA monitor and test chickens that go into grocery stores to ensure that they do not contain harmful antibiotic residue.

A label of "No Antibiotics Ever" or "Raised without Antibiotics" means that the chicken was never treated in its life with antibiotics. Usually a company has a line of animals that they will not treat with antibiotics if they get sick. If the chicken becomes so sick that it needs antibiotics, then it can no longer be marketed or labeled as "No Antibiotics Ever" or "Raised without Antibiotics."

NUTRITION LOWDOWN

The nutrition information for rotisserie chickens do differ between brands, so be sure to check the food label. Rotisserie chicken is an excellent source of niacin, phosphorus and selenium, and provides smaller amounts of vitamin B_{12} and pantothenic acid.

The nutritional difference between skin-on chicken and skinless chicken is significant, but both are free of carbohydrates, sugar and fiber. All rotisserie chickens are sold with the skin on (that's what keeps them moist); at home you can remove the skin if you choose. Three ounces (85 g) of rotisserie chicken with the skin and seasoning provides 219 calories, 19.5 grams of protein, 16 grams of fat, 4.2 grams of saturated fat and 7 grams of monounsaturated fat. Three ounces (85 g) of rotisserie chicken without the skin and seasoning provides 172 calories, 21 grams of protein, 10 grams of fat, 2.4 grams of saturated fat and 4 grams of monounsaturated fat. Just by removing the skin you can decrease the calories by about 20 percent and decrease the saturated fat by over 40 percent. If you are looking to reduce your dietary saturated fat, consider removing most or all of the skin from your bird. It's a healthier choice and quite easy to do.

The sodium of a rotisserie chicken is on the higher end for 3 ounces (85 g) of chicken, on average 500 to 550 mg (depending on how it's flavored, it can be more or less). If sodium is a concern, then opt for the non-flavored birds. You can always make your own sauce or condiment to accompany the bird. That way you are in better control of the ingredients.

DARK VERSES WHITE MEAT

Rotisserie chickens are smaller birds, so you really can't separate the dark meat (thighs and drumsticks) from the white meat (breast and wings). It is also more budget-friendly to eat the entire bird. On average, 3 ounces (85 g) of skinless, boneless chicken breast provides 92 calories, 19.5 grams of protein and 1 gram of fat with almost no saturated fat, while 3 ounces (85 g) of skinless dark meat provides 105 calories, 17 grams of protein, 4 grams of fat and about 1 gram of saturated fat. In other words, dark meat doesn't contain significantly more calories or saturated fat compared to white meat. It you're looking to avoid saturated fat, it is really the skin, not dark meat, you want to skip.

Now that you have a better understanding of how a rotisserie chicken is raised and its nutrient composition, it's time to select your bird and get cooking.

CHAPTER 2
COOKING MADE EASY

Picking up a rotisserie chicken during a busy workweek is an easy way to get dinner on the table in a flash. It can help free up time to spend with your loved ones or to take for yourself and it makes cooking a little less messy. The beauty of a rotisserie chicken is that it's ready to eat right off the bone, but that can get a little tiresome after a while. That is why it's helpful to have on hand a collection of simple, enticing recipes that utilize a rotisserie chicken to shave off prepping and cooking time.

HOW MANY CHICKENS SHOULD YOU BUY?

If you are buying a rotisserie chicken to serve as a main entrée, most birds have 4 cups (1 L) of meat, which makes four servings for a main dish. If you are serving one or two people, one bird is plenty. For a family of four, one bird will provide one serving of meat for each person. However, if you want to have leftovers or if you have growing teenagers in your home, buying two birds is a good idea. You can always double a recipe that serves four so you can have leftovers for the next day.

Typically, one rotisserie chicken will provide between 3½ cups (875 mL) and 4½ cups (1.125 L) of meat per bird, no matter which bird you choose. Costco is the only store I have found that has larger chickens that yield closer to 7 cups (1.75 L) of meat per bird (as their birds grow for slightly longer than typical rotisserie chickens).

REMOVING THE MEAT

Regardless of how you remove the meat from the bones of a rotisserie chicken, you want to get the most meat possible. I like to pull and shred the meat right from the breast (which is at the top of the chicken) without any rhyme or reason. My twelve-year-old helps me, and she has an easy time with this technique. I just always make sure the small bones have been removed.

If you prefer a more structured way to carve the bird, you can do the following:

TO BEGIN: Place the rotisserie chicken on a clean cutting board with the breast side facing up. Cut any string or twine that is holding the legs together.

SEPARATE THE LEGS: Pull one of the legs slightly away from the chicken and, using a sharp knife, slowly slice through the leg meat. Pull back on the leg and you'll find the hip joint. Pull with a bit of force until the hip bone pops up from the joint. Place your knife between the hip bone and the rest of the chicken and cut down until you can pull off the leg. You can opt to separate the drumstick and thigh into two pieces by finding the joint between the two pieces and cutting through with your knife.

MOVE TO THE BREAST: Using your knife, cut a line from the center of the breastbone at the front of the breast cavity to the back of the chicken. Pull the breast meat away from the bone while you are cutting. Repeat for the other breast.

REMOVE THE WINGS: Remove the wings, which are usually attached to the breast meat.

This cookbook calls for the meat of the chicken (as opposed to the parts of the chicken), either shredded or chopped into small pieces. Use whichever technique works best for you.

Please note that rotisserie chicken tends to have small bones. When removing meat from the bones, check that you didn't grab any bones along with the meat, or cut the meat into small pieces so you can identify and toss any bones.

COOKING FOR ONE

A rotisserie chicken is a pretty small bird that is a smart choice if you are cooking for one. You will probably get four servings of meat from the bird and have leftovers for a few days. If you are cooking for yourself, here are seven general tips to keep in mind.

SEVEN TIPS FOR COOKING FOR ONE

1. **Plan your meals ahead.** When you're cooking for yourself, using all the ingredients you have on hand is a worthwhile goal. It will help reduce food waste as well as how much you spend on your meals. When you plan ahead, you can select recipes that use similar ingredients to ensure everything gets used up. This is especially helpful with perishable foods, like fruits and vegetables, that spoil more quickly.

2. **Make a shopping list.** Shopping lists help minimize impulse purchases. Set a limit for yourself on the number of items you can purchase "off list." I restrict myself to no more than two items. Group the foods on your shopping list according to the way they are sold; for example, list all the fresh vegetables and fruit in one section. This will save you time at the store and help prevent you from forgetting an ingredient (which is always at the other end of the store).

3. **Don't forget frozen and canned.** Fresh fruit and vegetables have a short shelf life. When cooking for one, this can mean tossing out fresh produce that just never got used or eaten. Frozen and canned foods can help minimize food waste and can be just as healthy. Look for frozen fruit with no added sugar, where the fruit is the only ingredient, and frozen vegetables without added butter or sauces, where the vegetable is the only ingredient. Look for canned fruit in water or its own juices (extra light syrup can work, too) and canned vegetables that are low in sodium or with no added sodium. If you can only find full-sodium vegetables and beans, then rinse them before using. Research shows that up to 40 percent of the sodium in canned beans is removed when you rinse them.

4. **Cut a large recipe in half.** If you find that the yield of a recipe is just too much, cut it in half. You can also opt to make full recipes that freeze well, and then freeze half for a later date.

5. **Keep cooked foods front and center.** So that you don't forget about your cooked meals or extra ingredients, don't hide them in the refrigerator. Instead, put them front and center on your refrigerator shelf so you can remember to eat them or use them in future recipes. For example, if you have half a bell pepper left over from a recipe, you can use it in your morning omelet or slice it up to eat alongside a sandwich.

6. **Dinner for lunch.** You can get a good four meals out of your rotisserie chicken by packing leftovers for lunch the next day. It can help save you money and have your officemates drooling over your culinary creations.

7. **Get Creative.** Switch up the way you enjoy your rotisserie chicken. Leftover chicken can be eaten hot or cold. Top a salad, put it in a sandwich or toss it into a soup — and that's only the beginning.

COOKING FOR ONE: DO'S AND DON'TS

- **Do** plan your meals for the week. Remember to include eating leftovers and plan for meals where you will be dining out or eating at work.
- **Do** buy one rotisserie chicken when cooking for one.
- **Don't** buy two or three chickens and save them for later. The rotisserie chicken is only good for a few days.
- **Do** consider shopping in bulk with a friend. This is a good way to save money and split larger packaged items in order to minimize food waste.
- **Don't** overbuy ingredients to be saved for later. Ingredients like spices and nuts may seem smart to buy in larger quantities, but you're most likely to have them sitting in your pantry for years (*yes*, years!). The longer the food sits there, the more the quality and flavor will decrease.
- **Do** scale recipes in half if you think you won't be able to finish it on your own, especially if it won't freeze well.
- **Don't** scale large recipes serving eight or ten people down for one person. Downscaling the ingredients too much can throw the recipe off, resulting in a less than tasty dish.
- **Do** look for recipes that can be cooked and frozen for later. That can help minimize food waste.
- **Don't** freeze extra food in one large container. Instead, individually portion recipes so you can easily thaw, heat and eat.

FIVE BEST MEALS FOR SINGLE COOKS

Cooking for one can get frustrating if the recipe is tough to scale or cut in half. Here are five meals that are perfect when you are cooking for yourself.

Meal #1: Soup and Salad
Pair the Hearty Root Vegetable and Chicken Soup (page 63) with a green salad topped with Simple Balsamic Vinaigrette (page 172). This soup also freezes well, so you can cook a batch and freeze individual portions for another week.

Meal #2: Chicken Ranch Wrap
The Chicken Ranch Wrap (page 79) is easy to scale back for one person. Enjoy with a piece of fresh fruit, like an orange, pear or apple, on the side.

Meal #3: Hearty Salad
Scale down the Soba Noodle Salad (page 89) by cutting the ingredient amounts in half. You can enjoy it for dinner one night and lunch the next day.

Meal #4: Pesto Pasta with Chicken
The Pesto Pasta with Chicken (page 126) is a perfect recipe to cook and freeze for later. Enjoy two portions over three days, and freeze the remaining two portions individually.

Meal #5: Chicken Two Ways
The Lemon and Garlic Skillet Chicken (page 146) can be enjoyed hot or cold. When you cook it up, enjoy it warm served with Honey Roasted Carrots (page 158). Use the cold leftover chicken to top a green salad or in a sandwich.

COOKING FOR COUPLES

When cooking for two, you still need to control how much food you cook at once to help minimize food being tossed out. Here are some helpful tips if you are cooking for a couple.

SEVEN TIPS FOR COOKING FOR COUPLES

1. **Use smaller cookware and halve the recipe.** To help cut back portions, use smaller cookware, like smaller loaf pans for two-person meatloaf or casseroles. Cutting the recipe in half will allow the food to fit in the smaller cookware.

2. **Look for recipes that serve four.** These recipes are perfect for couples, as each person can get two servings. If someone needs more food, there is always extra on the table, or you can save the extra portions for lunch or dinner the next day.

3. **Freeze for later.** If you prepare recipes that are for eight or ten people, cook it all and then freeze half for later. Freezing double portions in one container is smart if you will be eating them together.

4. **Make simple substitutions.** Some perishable ingredients, like fresh herbs, may not be ideal in your two-person household. Substituting dried herbs for fresh may be a good idea and can save you a few dollars. Also, instead of buying a whole container of buttermilk for a recipe, add a little bit of fresh lemon juice to milk to create a buttermilk substitute.

5. **Use your freezer wisely.** Oftentimes extra ingredients can be frozen and used later. Shredded cheese, for example, can be frozen in sealable plastic bags, fresh herbs can be chopped and put into ice cubes trays mixed with a little water and reconstituted for recipes, and extra broth can also be portioned out and frozen in ice cube trays, then stashed in a sealable plastic bag until you're ready to use them.

6. **Scale back on fresh produce.** Fresh fruits and vegetables are certainly important, but they are also easy to overbuy. Instead, look for smaller portions of fresh produce or pick up a container of precut vegetables or fruit from the salad bar.

7. **Opt for frozen and canned produce.** With a longer shelf life, both frozen and canned fruits and vegetables can have a healthy place in your diet. Look for frozen fruit with no added sugar, where the fruit is the only ingredient, and frozen vegetables without added butter or sauces, again where the vegetable is the only ingredient. Look for canned fruit in water or its own juices (extra light syrup can work too) and canned vegetables that are low in sodium or with no added sodium. If you can only find full-sodium vegetables and beans, then rinse before using.

COOKING FOR COUPLES: DO'S AND DON'TS

- **Don't** eat out every night of the week. It's so easy to head out to the closest restaurant or fast-food joint to grab a quick bite to eat. But when you eat out, you don't have full control over the ingredients and the nutrition in your meals. Using a rotisserie chicken in a recipe is one way to quickly get home-cooked meals on the table.

- **Do** shop for two people. To help keep your spending under control, make a shopping list and stick to it.
- **Don't** purchase too many perishable items in one week. It's likely they will end up in the garbage. Canned and frozen items can help you get your daily recommended amount of fruits and vegetables.
- **Do** shop weekly. This will help you gauge how much you have in your kitchen so that you buy only what you need. It's also smart to buy perishable items weekly to prevent overbuying and waste.
- **Do** buy one rotisserie chicken. You will get about 4 cups (1 L) of chicken off the bone, which is perfect for two people.
- **Do** enjoy leftovers for lunch. When cooking for two, look for recipes that serve four or six and pack leftovers to tote to work for lunch.
- **Don't** keep all the leftovers in the refrigerator. If you're cooking a larger recipe, pack leftovers in individual or double portions and freeze until a later date. This will help minimize food being thrown out.
- **Do** taste what you're cooking so you can adjust the ingredients to your liking. Because you're only cooking for two people, it's easy to adjust recipes to fit everyone's likes and dislikes. Tasting your food as you prepare it can help make sure you have just enough salt and black pepper, for example.

FIVE BEST MEALS FOR COUPLES

If you're looking for delicious meals to cook for couples, here are five ideas to try. Pick up a rotisserie chicken and decide which you're going to whip up first.

Meal #1: Chili and Salad
Cook a batch of Sweet Potato Chicken Chili (page 109) and serve with a crispy green salad made with romaine lettuce, tomato, cucumber and bell peppers. Toss in Lemon-Herb Vinaigrette (page 171). Use leftovers for lunch the next day or freeze for a busy workweek.

Meal #2: Soup and Wrap
Make a new batch of Chicken Quinoa Soup (page 66) or use leftovers and serve with Curried Chicken and Pear Salad Wrap (page 73). Leftover chicken salad can be served over a green salad the next day with sliced oranges or mandarin oranges on the side.

Meal #3: A Hearty Salad
Pair the Brussels Sprouts Salad with Chicken, Cranberries and Pecans (page 90) with a simple berry medley for dessert (toss raspberries, sliced strawberries and blueberries in a bowl). Leftover salad holds up well in the fridge for a satisfying lunch the next day.

Meal #4: Balanced Bowls
Make Peanut Chicken and Quinoa Bowls with Broccoli (page 129), which are perfectly balanced meals with protein, whole grains and vegetables. Pair with diced melon for dessert. The recipe serves four, so you can pack two individual bowls for the next day.

Meal #5: Quesadillas
This recipe for Chicken, Spinach and Tomato Oven Quesadillas (page 140) is easy to halve to make only two servings. Serve with cut-up vegetables and guacamole on the side.

COOKING FOR FAMILIES

Family life is busy, and it can be tricky to make time to prepare a nutritious dinner each night. Luckily, buying a rotisserie chicken can help reduce time spent in the kitchen so that you can spend more time with your loved ones. Here are a few tips to keep in mind when cooking for your family to help make weeknight meals easier.

SEVEN TIPS FOR MAKING FAMILY MEALS EASY

1. **Meal plan.** Planning which meals to serve throughout the week for breakfast, lunch and dinner can help organize your life and answer the burning question your family keeps asking: "What's for dinner?" Post the schedule on your family board so everyone knows what is going to be served.

2. **Opt for healthy convenience food.** You have a lot of mouths to feed, so make your life easier by choosing convenience food that is healthy. Frozen fruits without added sugar and frozen vegetables with nothing additional in the ingredients list are healthy options. Frozen strawberries and peaches so easily whip up into a smoothie for breakfast or as a snack. Canned fruits in their own juices or water is an easy and healthy option, as are reduced-sodium canned beans and vegetables (or just rinse before using if you don't have a reduced-sodium option available). And of course, picking up a rotisserie chicken is another healthy convenience option that can help you get dinner on the table faster.

3. **Use time-saving kitchen tools.** Two of the most helpful tools in my kitchen are a vegetable chopper and a rice cooker (it also cooks up other whole grains), both of which are useful for recipes found in this book. Other appliances that help cut back on the amount of active time you spend making a meal include a slow cooker and a mini food processor (for chopping or grinding smaller items like nuts and bread crumbs).

4. **Make a double batch.** For highly requested recipes that serve four, double the recipe so you can have leftovers for a few days or freeze half for a busy week to come.

5. **Prep ahead of time.** It's a challenge to fully prep a meal after work and get it on the table in time for dinner during the week. Try prepping some of your ingredients the night before or in the morning before work.

6. **Get the kids involved.** Kids are more likely to enjoy the food if they are part of the cooking process. Younger kids, like toddlers, can help carry packaged foods or pour premeasured amounts of ingredients into mixing bowls, while older kids can help with selecting recipes, slicing, grating, mixing, setting the table and even cleaning up.

7. **Keep dinner simple.** There's no need to struggle for hours over a hot stove, creating a gourmet masterpiece. Choose recipes that are easy and quick to make. Once you find a handful of recipes that everyone loves, it's easy to prepare them over and over.

COOKING FOR FAMILIES: DO'S AND DON'TS

- **Don't** cook blindly. Opening your refrigerator when you get home and deciding last minute what's for dinner will have you ordering delivery more often than not. Have a schedule for your meals and plan ahead.
- **Do** keep a well-stocked kitchen. Having ingredients stashed in your pantry, like herbs, canned goods, nuts, grains and stock, can help minimize time in the grocery store.
- **Do** meal prep for the week. When cooking for a family, cooking several meals at the beginning of the week can minimize how much you cook each evening.
- **Don't** serve the same thing daily. Even if you cook large batches of foods, don't serve them the same way every night — that gets boring! Instead, get a little creative and repurpose your food. For example, the White Bean and Chicken Chili (page 130) can be repurposed as quesadillas and the Skillet Balsamic Chicken (page 154) can be used on a pizza with tomato sauce and mozzarella cheese.
- **Do** learn to multitask in the kitchen. Preparing several recipes at once can take a lot of time, unless you learn to multitask. When you have 10 or 15 minutes while one recipe is cooking, take that time to prepare the dressing or chop vegetables for the next dish. It takes a little practice, but once you get the hang of multitasking in the kitchen, you'll be glad you learned!
- **Don't** throw away extra ingredients. For example, use leftover rotisserie chicken for breakast, like in Chicken and Vegetable Breakfast Frittata (page 37), or for snacks, like Easy Chicken Zucchini Boats (page 53).

FIVE BEST MEALS FOR FAMILIES

Meal #1: Pizza and Salad
Pair the Hawaiian Chicken Pizza (page 143) with a large green salad made with romaine lettuce, tomatoes, mushrooms, shredded carrots and cucumbers and Easy Ranch Dressing (page 174). Double the pizza recipe, if needed, which will yield two pizzas.

Meal #2: Taco Tuesday
Whip up these Weeknight Chicken Soft Tacos (page 132) or make a taco bar with the ingredients and have your family assemble their own. Serve with optional toppings, which include salsa, sour cream (or Greek yogurt) and guacamole.

Meal #3: Spaghetti and Meatballs
Cook a batch of Herbed Chicken Meatballs (page 136) and stir them into your favorite warmed store-bought or homemade pasta sauce. Serve over the pasta of your choice and alongside Sheet Pan Vegetables (page 160).

Meal #4: Lasagna
Whip up an easy Chicken and Cheese Lasagna (page 104) and serve with steamed broccoli and crusty bread on the side.

Meal #5: Mac and Cheese
Give your crew an extra boost of satisfying protein in this Mac and Cheese with Chicken (page 102). Serve with Honey Roasted Carrots (page 158) on the side.

MEALS READY IN 15 MINUTES OR LESS

Purchasing a rotisserie chicken can make cooking simple — and quick! So much so that you can even find meals that can make it on your table in 15 minutes or less.

SEVEN TIPS FOR GETTING MEALS ON THE TABLE IN 15 MINUTES OR LESS

1. **Preshred your rotisserie chicken.** You can save a time at dinner by pulling the rotisserie chicken off the bone once you bring your chicken home or the night before you're planning to serve it.

2. **Prepare your *mis en place*.** This French culinary terms translates to "putting in place" or "everything in its place" and means to have all your ingredients chopped, diced, juiced, measured or anything else the recipe calls for. By getting the prep out of the way, all you need to do is toss together the ingredients for your dish as you follow the recipe.

3. **Go simple.** Getting meals on the table in 15 minutes or less means that you aren't cooking anything elaborate. If you do want to prepare a recipe that takes longer, shave off time by swapping time-intensive ingredients for time-saving ingredients. For example, instead of shredding whole, raw carrots, choose cherry tomatoes, which have no chopping or shredding involved. You can also opt for canned precut vegetables, instead of fresh that need more time to prep. Another example is using dried herbs and spices instead of chopping fresh herbs.

4. **Opt for hot sandwiches.** Heating up sandwiches takes them to a whole new level. Look to panini, grilled cheese or melts for a deliciously simple dinner. Add rotisserie chicken to each for a more satisfying meal.

5. **Look for a short list of ingredients.** A shorter ingredient list means less to measure and prepare. Keep an eye out for recipes in this book that are marked five ingredients or less.

6. **Keep frozen vegetables stocked.** Make an easy side dish using your favorite frozen vegetables, which take 5 minutes to prepare. Frozen veggies to the rescue!

7. **Get everyone involved.** The more hands you can get on board to help you, the quicker dinner will be done. However many you are cooking for, a little extra help goes a long way.

RECIPES IN 15 MINUTES OR LESS

- Mandarin Chicken Lettuce Cups (page 50)
- Chicken Avocado Toast (page 51)
- Easy Chicken Wrap (page 69)
- Grilled Apple, Gouda and Chicken Panini (page 70)
- BBQ Chicken Sliders (page 72)
- Chicken Shawarma Stuffed Pita (page 71)
- Curried Chicken and Pear Salad Wrap (page 73)
- Cajun Chicken Melt (page 77)

- Chipotle Chicken Grilled Cheese (page 78)
- Chicken Caprese Salad (page 82)
- Chicken, Peach and Goat Cheese Salad (page 92)
- Buffalo Chicken Salad (page 83)
- Chicken, Kale and White Bean Salad (page 93)
- Thai-Style Chicken Curry (page 128)
- Weeknight Chicken Soft Tacos (page 132)
- Chicken and Vegetable Stir-Fry (page 138)
- Lemon and Garlic Skillet Chicken (page 146)
- Chicken in Orange Sauce (page 153)
- Skillet Balsamic Chicken (page 154)

RECIPES WITH FIVE INGREDIENTS OR LESS

As a single working mother of three kids, I am always trying to simplify recipes in order to quickly get a meal on the table. One of the easiest ways to do so is to reduce the number of ingredients I am working with. Recipes with no more than five ingredients are flagged in this book, but you can also simplify any recipe by using only the basic ingredients to make it. Keep in mind that the kitchen staples — salt, black pepper, nonstick cooking spray and olive oil or canola oil — don't count toward the five ingredients.

FIVE TIPS FOR MAKING RECIPES WITH FIVE INGREDIENTS OR LESS

1. **Keep it super simple.** Instead of cooking meatballs with ten or twelve ingredients, scale the ingredients list down to the essentials. By the time you're done, the list will be about five ingredients long.

2. **Aim for a short shopping list.** Keeping recipes to five ingredients will help pare down your shopping list. That is also a good way to gauge if you're really sticking to five ingredients — that shopping list should be shorter than usual so you can get in and out of the grocery store in a flash.

3. **Eliminate extra ingredients.** Don't worry about garnishes like chopped cilantro or other recipe extras that are not necessary to create the dish. Although they are nice to have, when you are looking to simplify, getting a meal on the table is the priority.

4. **Use one cooking method.** Many recipes with multiple cooking methods also have many ingredients used (for each cooking method). A simple ingredient list also calls for simple cooking techniques — think one-pan meals.

5. **Use ingredients that combine flavors.** Instead of using individual herbs like basil, oregano, rosemary and thyme in one recipe, opt for dried Italian seasoning, which includes these herbs (plus marjoram) in one bottle. You can also use frozen mixed vegetables instead of individual vegetables or Sriracha mayonnaise instead of adding Sriracha and mayo separately.

ROTISSERIE CHICKEN RECIPES WITH FIVE INGREDIENTS OR LESS

- Easy Chicken Zucchini Boats (page 53)
- Chicken and Cheese Tortilla Pizza (page 54)
- Chicken Ranch Wrap (page 79)
- Basic Chicken Melt (page 75)
- Chicken Caprese Salad (page 82)
- Chicken, Kale and White Bean Salad (page 93)
- Chicken, Spinach and Tomato Oven Quesadilla (page 140)

SIDES, DRESSINGS, SAUCES AND CONDIMENTS WITH FIVE INGREDIENTS OR LESS

- Sheet Pan Broccoli and Cauliflower (page 160)
- Honey Roasted Carrots (page 158)
- Sautéed Zucchini with Lemon and Pine Nuts (page 161)
- Garlic Sautéed Spinach (page 163)
- Garlic Parmesan Quinoa (page 166)
- Cranberry-Almond Farro (page 167)
- Simple Balsamic Vinaigrette (page 172)
- Lemon-Herb Vinaigrette (page 171)
- Ginger Dressing (page 175)
- Tzatziki (page 179)
- Spicy Peanut Sauce (page 180)
- Hummus (page 181)

MEAL PREPPING

Take traditional meal planning a step further by preparing, cooking and boxing individual servings of one or more weekly meals or snacks. Meal prepping can be done for one, two or ten recipes — depending on your household's needs. How you plan your meal prepping is up to you. You can choose to meal prep one day a week (like Sunday) or you can meal prep two days during the week.

ADVANTAGES OF MEAL PREPPING

Meal prepping is something that I do regularly, and I even wrote two cookbooks on the topic. It has so many benefits, including:

1. **Save money.** Meal planning and prepping allows you to know how much you will need of each ingredient you are using, which helps minimize overbuying. This is especially helpful with more expensive items like cheese, fish and nuts.
2. **Save time.** Meal prepping once or twice a week helps save about 45 minutes on a work night. This extra time can be spent with loved ones or doing something kind for yourself, like attending an exercise class, watching a favorite show or even getting to bed earlier.

3. **Eat healthier.** By planning your week, you can select healthy recipes to prepare. The recipes in this cookbook are flagged when appropriate for meal prepping. When you have dinner boxed up and ready to eat, it will help minimize pit stops on the way home from work to the local fast-food joint, or last-minute orders online for delivery.

4. **Decrease stress.** Thinking about what to make for dinner can be extremely stressful. You have to think about the meal you want to cook, the ingredients you need to buy and how you will cook it. Meal prepping takes all the stress away, so you can focus your energy on other tasks that need to get done.

5. **Improve multitasking skills.** By learning to cook a few recipes at once, you'll start improving your ability to multitask in the kitchen. After some practice, you will become an expert, which will help you become more efficient at cooking in general. For example, if you are preparing a pot of chili, you can quickly whisk together a salad dressing in 5 to 10 minutes. Knowing how to multitask while cooking will help you get more done in less time.

DO'S AND DON'TS OF MEAL PREPPING

- **Do** meal prep at your own pace. You don't have to meal prep like the pros right out of the gate. Start with two or three recipes, and once you are comfortable with that many, slowly work your way up.

- **Don't** wait until the last minute to meal prep. The number one rule of meal prepping is planning. Without proper planning you won't be able to find your recipes, make a shopping list, go food shopping, prep, cook and box up all your meals.

- **Do** work within your own schedule. Which meals you prep is up to you. Some people need breakfast prepped for the week, while other people just want lunch and dinner prepped for the week. Do whatever works best for you.

- **Don't** skip on boxing up meals. An important step in meal prepping is to preportion individual meals. Without doing this, you may overserve yourself and be left with one less meal than you expected. And if one goal of meal prepping is to help with weight loss or maintenance, it's easier to overconsume portions and calories if you don't box your meal.

- **Do** freeze extras. You may have one or more extra servings that can be frozen, like lasagna or chili. Box them into individual portions and freeze for a later date.

- **Don't** overprep. Although meal prepping can help minimize food waste and save you time, making too many meals can sabotage these efforts. When you prepare too much food, you can end up with extras that get tossed once too many days have passed.

FIVE STEPS TO MEAL PREPPING

**I like to break down meal prepping into five easy steps.
These steps will help keep you organized and
on track with your meal prepping efforts.**

1. **Choose when to prep.** Schedule your day or days and time to meal prep. Determine if you want to meal prep one day of the week (like on Sundays) or divide meal prepping into two days (like Sundays and Wednesdays). If you like to have a lot of fresh produce on hand, think about meal prepping over two days instead of once a week.

2. **Determine which meals to prep.** Decide how many meals you want to prep for the week ahead. Do you want to prepare only breakfasts and dinners? Or some other combination of meals? Remember to take into account nights you may have dinner plans or mornings you may have a breakfast meeting. When selecting your meals, don't forget to include all the food groups in your day, including fruits, vegetables, dairy, starches (especially whole grains) and protein. There are many recipes in this cookbook that you can meal prep. If there is no vegetable or grain in the dish, then select meal prep sides from chapter 9 to include in your meal.

3. **Go food shopping.** Once you select your recipes, sit in your kitchen with a blank sheet of paper or your notes section on your smartphone or tablet and list all the ingredients you need. Double-check your kitchen inventory for all ingredients to make sure you are not buying items you already have in your pantry. I like to organize my grocery list by the flow of the market I am buying from, which usually starts with fresh fruits and vegetables. This helps make food shopping quick and easy, and minimizes the likelihood of forgetting an item until I'm in the other end of the store.

4. **Prep and cook.** Organize your recipes so you know when to chop and prepare ingredients and when to cook. As a general rule, I like to cook the recipes that require baking or roasting first and prep condiments, sauces or dressings during a 10- or 15-minute break when a dish is in the oven.

5. **Portion and box.** This is an important step that should never be skipped. Portioning and boxing your prepared food into individual servings or meals helps ensure that you will have enough food for all your planned meals. As a general rule, I like each box to consist of one-quarter protein, one-quarter starches (especially whole grains) and one-half vegetables or fruit. If you ever feel like you need more food, increase the portion of your vegetables. You can choose to portion and box your meals in a container that has several segments or in one big container where the food can mix together.

CHOOSING YOUR MEAL PREP CONTAINERS

When you begin to meal prep, you will need some containers to pack your meals. Do not stock up on one type of container before you've experimented and weighed the pros and cons. Here are a few things to keep in mind when selecting your meal prep containers.

- **Single space or multiple compartments.** Like I mentioned before, some people prefer all their food in one larger compartment, while other like a few smaller compartments so the food doesn't touch. That is a personal preference.
- **Stackability.** If you continue to meal prep, you will accumulate a collection of containers. Stackable containers help save space when not in use and keep you organized.
- **BPA-free.** The chemical bisphenol A (BPA) has been around since the 1960s, and although BPA in plastic food storage containers has been found to be safe in small amounts for frequent use, many consumers prefer to purchase them BPA-free. Look on the package where it should be noted that the containers are "BPA-free." Glass containers do not contain BPA.
- **Leakproof.** The last thing you want is to arrive at work with your lunch leaking all over the place. Before purchasing containers, read the online reviews carefully to determine if they leak or if the tops easily come off. Initially buy one or two and test them out. See how they do when in your car, on the bus or any other way that you travel daily.
- **Microwave, oven, dishwasher and freezer safe.** You want your meal prep containers to be as versatile as possible. Containers may need to be frozen, reheated in the oven or microwave and cleaned in the dishwasher. Read the label carefully to make sure where you can and cannot use the meal prep containers before buying.

FIFTEEN BEST RECIPES FOR MEAL PREPPING

- Hearty Root Vegetable and Chicken Soup (page 63)
- Pesto Pasta with Chicken (page 126)
- Mediterranean Orzo and Chicken (page 127)
- Spanish-Style Chicken with Peppers and Olives (page 151)
- Chicken and Vegetable Stew (page 96)
- Chicken and Cheese Lasagna (page 104)
- Southwest Chicken and Rice Stuffed Peppers (page 112)
- Greek Chicken and Rice Bowls (page 116)
- Mac and Cheese with Chicken (page 102)
- Sweet Potato Chicken Chili (page 109)
- Chicken Fajita Bowls (page 115)
- Chicken Parmesan Casserole (page 97)
- Chicken and Mushroom Baked Risotto (page 108)
- Chicken and Spinach Stuffed Shells (page 106)
- North African Chicken and Quinoa (page 114)

CHAPTER 3

BREAKFAST

CRUSTLESS SPINACH, CHEESE AND CHICKEN QUICHE

Quiches are a perfect way to use leftover vegetables, the last bit of that block of cheese and, of course, leftover rotisserie chicken. Try kale instead of spinach, and chopped broccoli or cauliflower and shredded carrots work well in this recipe.

PREHEAT THE OVEN TO 425°F (220°C)

Nonstick cooking spray

5 large eggs, beaten

4 large egg whites, beaten

½ cup (125 mL) milk

¼ tsp (1 mL) salt

⅛ tsp (0.5 mL) freshly ground black pepper

1 tbsp (15 mL) olive oil or canola oil

1 yellow onion, chopped

1 clove garlic, minced

3 cups (750 mL) packed baby spinach, chopped

1½ cups (375 mL) rotisserie chicken, finely chopped

1 cup (250 mL) shredded Cheddar cheese

1. Coat an 8-inch (20 cm) pie plate with nonstick cooking spray.

2. In a medium bowl, whisk together the eggs, egg whites, milk, salt and pepper.

3. Heat the oil in a medium skillet over medium heat. When the oil is shimmering, add the onion and garlic and cook, stirring occasionally, until the onion is translucent and the garlic is fragrant, 3 minutes. Add the spinach and cook, stirring occasionally, until the spinach has wilted, 3 minutes more.

4. Spread the spinach mixture on the bottom of the prepared pie plate, top evenly with the chicken and sprinkle with the cheese. Pour the egg mixture evenly over the top. Bake in the preheated oven until the top has browned and a knife inserted about 1 inch (2.5 cm) from the edge comes out clean, about 35 minutes. Cut into eight even slices. Serve warm.

SERVING SIZE: ⅛ quiche

TOBY'S TIPS: Lighten it up by using 2% milk and reduced-fat cheese.

One of my favorite time-saving kitchen tools is a vegetable chopper. It's inexpensive and cuts food into same-size pieces.

CHICKEN AND VEGETABLE BREAKFAST FRITTATA

Adding vegetables to your breakfast is an easy way to help you meet the recommended daily requirement. You can also substitute leftover vegetables in the fridge to minimize food waste in your home. Chopped broccoli, cauliflower, asparagus and mushrooms all work well in this recipe.

PREHEAT THE BROILER
OVENPROOF SKILLET

4 large eggs, beaten

½ tsp (2 mL) dried parsley

½ tsp (2 mL) dried oregano

½ tsp (2 mL) salt

⅛ tsp (1 mL) freshly ground black pepper

1 tbsp (15 mL) olive oil or canola oil

1 yellow onion, chopped

1 clove garlic, minced

1 cup (250 mL) finely chopped rotisserie chicken

1 carrot, shredded

1 cup (250 mL) cherry tomatoes, halved lengthwise

1 zucchini, sliced lengthwise and then cut into ½-inch (1 cm) half-moons

¾ cup (175 mL) shredded mozzarella cheese

1. In a medium bowl, whisk the eggs, parsley, oregano, salt and pepper.

2. Heat the oil in an ovenproof skillet over medium heat. When the oil is shimmering, add the onion and garlic and cook until the onion is translucent, 3 minutes. Add the chicken, carrot, tomatoes and zucchini and cook until the vegetables soften, about 5 minutes. Reduce the heat to medium-low. Add the egg mixture and cover, allowing the eggs to settle and cook through, 10 minutes.

3. Sprinkle the eggs with the cheese and place the skillet under the preheated broiler. Cook until the cheese has melted and is slightly browned, 2 minutes. Cut into six even slices.

SERVING SIZE: ⅙ frittata

TOBY'S TIP: Shredded part-skim mozzarella cheese is a go-to in my house. I divide a large bag into sealable containers to store in the freezer.

NOT YOUR MAMA'S CHICKEN AND WAFFLES

Chicken for breakfast? Yes! For a simple, easy-to-make spin-off of the typical fried chicken and waffles, use rotisserie chicken. Here, shredded rotisserie chicken is served in a white gravy over a homemade waffle.

PREHEAT WAFFLE IRON
STANDARD WAFFLE MAKER, COATED WITH NONSTICK COOKING SPRAY

WAFFLES

Nonstick cooking spray

2 cups (250 mL) unbleached all-purpose flour

1 tbsp (15 mL) baking powder

1 tsp (5 mL) salt

1½ cups (375 mL) milk

½ cup (125 mL) unsweetened applesauce

2 large eggs, beaten

2 tbsp (30 mL) pure maple syrup

2 tbsp (30 mL) canola oil

1 tsp (5 mL) vanilla extract

CHICKEN

2 tbsp (30 mL) unsalted butter

3 tbsp (45 mL) unbleached all-purpose flour

¼ tsp (1 mL) paprika

¼ tsp (1 mL) ground thyme

⅛ tsp (0.5 mL) cayenne pepper

⅛ tsp (0.5 mL) salt

⅛ tsp (0.5 mL) freshly ground black pepper

¾ cup (175 mL) reduced-sodium ready-to-use chicken broth

¾ cup (175 mL) milk

3 cups (750 mL) shredded rotisserie chicken

1. **WAFFLES:** In a medium bowl, sift together the flour, baking powder and salt.

2. In a separate medium bowl, whisk together the milk, applesauce, eggs, maple syrup, oil and vanilla extract. Gently fold the dry ingredients into the wet ingredients, being careful not to overmix.

continued on next page

3. Spoon 1 cup (250 mL) of the waffle mixture into the preheated waffle iron. Cook until golden brown, about 6 minutes (or per manufacturer's instructions), and place the cooked waffle on a plate. Cover with a clean cloth or paper towel and repeat for the remaining waffle for a total of two waffles.

4. CHICKEN: Heat the butter in a medium skillet over medium heat. When the butter is melted, sprinkle with the flour, paprika, thyme, cayenne, salt and black pepper; stir for 1 minute. Add the chicken broth and milk and stir to combine. Raise the heat to high and bring the mixture to a boil, stirring occasionally. Lower the heat to medium-low and simmer, gently whisking until slightly thickened, 3 minutes. Add the chicken and toss to evenly coat. Continue cooking, stirring occasionally, until the chicken is warmed through, 2 minutes.

5. ASSEMBLE: Slice each waffle in half. Spoon $\frac{1}{2}$ cup (125 mL) of the chicken and gravy over each waffle half and serve warm.

MAKE AHEAD: The waffles can be prepared ahead of time and stored in the refrigerator for up to 4 days. Reheat in the toaster or toaster oven.

SERVING SIZE: $\frac{1}{2}$ waffle and approximately $\frac{1}{2}$ cup (125 mL) chicken

TOBY'S TIPS: When buying maple syrup, look for pure maple syrup, which may be labeled "pure," "100%" or "100% pure." Maple syrup will be the only ingredient. Other maple-like syrups are made with corn syrup and artificial ingredients.

•

To increase the whole grains in the waffle, swap 1 cup (250 mL) of the all-purpose flour for whole wheat pastry flour. Lighten up the recipe by using 2% milk.

HUEVOS RANCHEROS
WITH CHICKEN

Every time I travel down South, one of the must-have dishes I order is huevos rancheros. Instead of waiting for my trips in order to enjoy this scrumptious dish, I can make my own just the way I like it — and now you can too!

1 tbsp (15 mL) olive oil

1 yellow onion, chopped

1 clove garlic, minced

4½-oz (127 mL) can chopped green chiles, with juice

1 cup (250 mL) drained canned reduced-sodium black beans

1½ cups (375 mL) finely chopped rotisserie chicken

14-oz (398 mL) can fire-roasted crushed tomatoes, with juice

1 tsp (5 mL) ground cumin

¼ tsp (1 mL) salt, divided

⅛ tsp (0.5 mL) cayenne pepper

4 large eggs

Four 8-inch (20 cm) flour tortillas

½ cup (125 mL) shredded Mexican blend cheese

2 tbsp (30 mL) chopped fresh cilantro

1. Heat the oil in a large skillet over medium heat. When the oil is shimmering, add the onion and garlic and cook until the onion is translucent and the garlic is fragrant, 3 minutes. Add the green chiles with juice, black beans and chicken and cook until heated through, 5 minutes. Add the crushed tomatoes with juice, cumin, ⅛ tsp (0.5 mL) of the salt and cayenne; toss to combine. Raise the heat to high and bring the mixture to a boil. Lower the heat to medium. Using the back of a spoon, make four wells in the sauce. Carefully break open an egg into each well and sprinkle the eggs with the remaining salt. Cover the skillet and cook until the eggs are heated through, 10 minutes.

2. Place a tortilla onto each of four large plates. Spoon over one-quarter of the chicken and egg mixture and top with 2 tbsp (30 mL) of the cheese and ½ tbsp (22 mL) of the cilantro.

SERVING SIZE: 1 plate

TOBY'S TIPS: Lighten up this recipe by using reduced-fat shredded Mexican blend cheese. Use whole wheat tortillas to increase the fiber.

•

Dress up your huevos rancheros with salsa, sliced avocado and hot sauce.

ROTISSERIE CHICKEN BREAKFAST BURRITOS

Start your day with this Mexican-inspired burrito filled with eggs, rotisserie chicken, chile peppers and Jack cheese. Enjoy for lunch or dinner, too!

Nonstick cooking spray

Four 8-inch (20 cm) flour tortillas

5 large eggs

¼ cup (60 mL) milk

¼ tsp (1 mL) salt

⅛ tsp (0.5 mL) freshly ground black pepper

1 tbsp (15 mL) olive oil

1 cup (250 mL) shredded rotisserie chicken

4½-oz (127 mL) can diced green chiles, with juice

1 tsp (5 mL) ground cumin

½ tsp (2 mL) ground coriander

½ cup (125 mL) shredded Monterey Jack cheese

½ cup (125 mL) Chunky Salsa (page 182) or store-bought salsa

1. Coat a medium skillet with nonstick cooking spray and heat over medium-low heat. Place a tortilla in the warmed skillet and heat for 30 seconds on each side. Transfer the warmed tortilla to a large plate, lay it flat and cover with a paper towel or clean kitchen towel. Repeat with the remaining tortillas.

2. In a medium bowl, whisk the eggs, milk, salt and pepper.

3. Coat the same skillet with nonstick cooking spray and heat over medium heat. When the oil is shimmering, pour in the egg mixture. Using a spatula, fold and invert the eggs until large, soft curds form, about 3 minutes. Place the egg mixture onto a clean plate. Wipe the inside of the skillet with a clean paper towel.

4. Heat the oil in the same skillet over medium heat. When the oil is shimmering, add the chicken, chile peppers with juice, cumin and coriander. Toss to evenly coat and continue cooking until the chicken is warmed through, about 3 minutes.

5. To assemble, place a warmed tortilla on a flat surface. Add one-quarter of the egg mixture, ¼ cup (60 mL) of the chicken mixture and 2 tbsp (30 mL) each of the cheese and salsa. Fold the bottom edge of each tortilla up and over the filling, fold in the opposite sides and roll up from the bottom. Repeat for the remaining burritos.

SERVING SIZE: 1 burrito

TOBY'S TIP: Lighten up the recipe with whole wheat tortillas, 4 large eggs and 2 large egg whites, skim milk and reduced-fat cheese.

CHICKEN AND EGG HASH

Potatoes are a powerhouse ingredient packed with a variety of nutrients. One medium potato provides 110 calories, 3 grams of protein and 2 grams of fiber and is an excellent source of the antioxidant vitamin C. It also has more potassium than a banana!

1 tbsp (15 mL) olive oil or canola oil

1 yellow onion, chopped

1 clove garlic, minced

2 russet potatoes (about 1 lb/500 g), peeled and diced into ½-inch (1 cm) cubes

1 red bell pepper, chopped

⅓ cup (75 mL) water

1 cup (250 mL) finely shredded rotisserie chicken

1 tsp (5 mL) smoked paprika

½ tsp (2 mL) dried oregano

¼ tsp (1 mL) cayenne pepper

¼ tsp (1 mL) salt, divided

⅛ tsp (0.5 mL) freshly ground black pepper

4 large eggs

1. Heat the oil in a large skillet over medium heat. When the oil is shimmering, add the onion and garlic and cook until the onion is translucent and the garlic is fragrant, 3 minutes. Add the potatoes, red pepper and water to the skillet and allow to cook, covered, until the potatoes are tender, 10 minutes. Add the chicken, paprika, oregano, cayenne, ⅛ tsp (0.5 mL) of the salt and black pepper. Cook, tossing occasionally, until the potatoes are browned and the chicken is warmed through, 5 to 7 minutes more.

2. Using the back of a spoon, make four wells in the hash. Carefully break one egg into each of the wells and sprinkle the eggs with the remaining salt. Cover the skillet and allow the eggs to cook through, 8 to 10 minutes.

SERVING SIZE: ¼ hash and 1 egg

TOBY'S TIP: Not used to cracking eggs? Crack one egg into a wineglass or small ramekin and then carefully pour it into the potato well. This way you can avoid getting eggshells in your dish.

APPETIZERS AND SNACKS

GAME DAY DIP

Watching the big game with family or friends? Whip up this warm dip made with rotisserie chicken and lots of cheese. Add more or less hot sauce, depending on the preferences of your guests, and serve it with celery sticks, carrot sticks, zucchini sticks or crackers.

PREHEAT THE OVEN TO 350°F (180°C)
1½-QUART (1.5 L) CASSEROLE DISH OR LARGE OVENPROOF RAMEKIN,
COATED WITH NONSTICK COOKING SPRAY

Nonstick cooking spray

3 cups (750 mL) finely shredded rotisserie chicken

½ cup (125 mL) hot pepper sauce

½ cup (125 mL) plain Greek yogurt

8 oz (225 g) whipped cream cheese

1 cup (250 mL) shredded Cheddar cheese

2 stalks celery, finely chopped

2 green onions, chopped

1. In a medium saucepan, heat the chicken and hot sauce. Cook until the chicken is heated through and has absorbed much of the sauce, about 5 minutes. Remove from heat, and allow chicken to cool slightly, about 5 minutes.

2. In a large bowl, combine the chicken, Greek yogurt, cream cheese, Cheddar cheese, celery and green onions. Mix to combine. Place the ingredients into the prepared casserole dish, evening out the top with the back of a spoon. Place the casserole dish in the preheated oven and bake until the top is slightly browned and bubbly, 20 to 25 minutes.

SERVING SIZE: ¼ cup (60 mL)

TOBY'S TIPS: Lighten up this dip by using nonfat plain Greek yogurt, Neufchâtel cheese in place of the cream cheese and reduced-fat shredded Cheddar cheese.

•

My favorite hot pepper sauces for this dish are Frank's RedHot Original and Cholula Hot Sauce.

CHICKEN AND TOMATO BRUSCHETTA

When serving this bruschetta, be warned — these babies will disappear in 5 minutes or less! I recommend making a double batch and serving them in two shifts.

PREHEAT THE OVEN TO 450°F (230°C)

Nonstick cooking spray

1 French baguette

2 tbsp (30 mL) olive oil

12 oz (340 g) plum (Roma) tomatoes (about 3), chopped

1 cup (250 mL) chopped rotisserie chicken

8 basil leaves, thinly sliced

2 cloves garlic, minced

3 tbsp (45 mL) extra virgin olive oil

½ tsp (2 mL) salt

⅛ tsp (0.5 mL) freshly ground black pepper

1. Coat a baking sheet with nonstick cooking spray.

2. Slice the baguette on the diagonal into about twenty-four ½-inch (1 cm) thick slices. Use a brush to coat both sides of the baguette slices with olive oil and bake in the preheated oven until the edges are slightly browned, 5 minutes. Remove from the oven and let the toast cool.

3. In a medium bowl, add the tomatoes, chicken, basil and garlic; toss to combine. Add the extra virgin olive oil, salt and pepper and toss evenly to coat.

4. Spoon 1 heaping tbsp (15 mL) of the tomato and chicken mixture onto each of the toasted baguette pieces. Place on a serving plate and serve immediately.

MAKE AHEAD: The tomato and chicken mixture can be made 1 day ahead of time.

SERVING SIZE: 3 pieces

TOBY'S TIPS: Use a whole wheat French baguette to make this appetizer a little healthier.

When buying fresh basil, look for bright green leaves without yellow or brown spots. Place cut stems in a container of water and keep on the windowsill for up to 1 week, changing the water daily. Fresh basil can also be stored in the refrigerator wrapped in a damp paper towel for 3 to 4 days.

CHICKEN STUFFED BAKED POTATO SKINS

Potato skins make a great finger food, especially for those messy younger eaters. To make this appetizer a little lighter (but just as delicious!), try using nonfat Greek yogurt instead of sour cream.

PREHEAT THE OVEN TO 400°F (200°C)

Nonstick cooking spray

4 russet potatoes

1 cup (250 mL) shredded Gruyère cheese (about 1½ oz/43 g)

¼ cup (60 mL) sour cream or plain Greek yogurt

½ tsp (2 mL) salt

⅛ tsp (0.5 mL) freshly ground black pepper

¼ cup (60 mL) red cooking wine or dry red wine

2 tsp (10 mL) Worcestershire sauce

1 tsp (5 mL) honey

½ tsp (2 mL) dried thyme

1 tbsp (15 mL) olive oil

1 clove garlic, minced

1 yellow onion, thinly sliced

1 cup (250 mL) chopped rotisserie chicken

1. Coat a baking sheet with nonstick cooking spray.

2. Pierce each potato several times with a fork. Place on the prepared baking sheet and bake in the preheated oven until tender, about 50 minutes. Remove from the oven and carefully slice the potatoes lengthwise and let cool for 10 minutes.

3. Preheat the broiler.

4. Scoop out the inside flesh of the potatoes, leaving about ¼ inch (0.5 cm) of flesh inside. Place the scooped-out potato in a medium bowl. Add the cheese, sour cream, salt and pepper and mash together using a potato masher or fork.

5. In a small bowl, whisk together the red wine, Worcestershire sauce, honey and thyme.

6. Heat the oil in a medium saucepan over medium heat. When the oil is shimmering, add the garlic and cook, stirring, until fragrant, 30 seconds. Add the onion and cook, stirring occasionally, until translucent and browned, 8 minutes. Add the red wine mixture and cook, stirring occasionally, until the liquid has evaporated, about 3 minutes. Add the chicken and toss to combine. Cook, stirring occasionally, until the chicken is heated through, 2 minutes.

7. To serve, evenly divide the onion mixture between the 8 potato halves and spoon the potato mixture over the onions. Place the potato halves onto the prepared baking sheet and heat under the broiler until the top is slightly browned, 2 minutes.

SERVING SIZE: 1 potato skin

TOBY'S TIP: Lighten up the dish by swapping the Gruyère cheese for part-skim mozzarella or reduced-fat extra-sharp (old) Cheddar or Jack cheese, and use nonfat sour cream or nonfat plain Greek yogurt.

MANDARIN CHICKEN LETTUCE CUPS

This spin on chicken salad uses mandarin oranges, almonds and green onions. The sweet and savory combination is always a hit with family and friends. You can also serve the chicken salad on cucumber or zucchini rounds or whole wheat crackers for a simple but tasty appetizer.

¼ cup (60 mL) mayonnaise

¼ cup (60 mL) plain Greek yogurt

2 tsp (10 mL) reduced-sodium soy sauce

1 tsp (5 mL) freshly squeezed lemon juice

⅛ tsp (0.5 mL) freshly ground black pepper

3 cups (750 mL) chopped rotisserie chicken

⅓ cup (80 mL) unsalted roasted almonds, chopped

1 cup (250 mL) canned mandarin oranges in 100% fruit juice or water, drained and roughly chopped

2 green onions, chopped

12 leaves lettuce (preferably Bibb lettuce)

1. In a small bowl, whisk together the mayonnaise, Greek yogurt, soy sauce, lemon juice and pepper.

2. In a medium bowl, add the chicken, almonds, mandarin oranges and green onions; toss to combine. Add the mayonnaise dressing and toss to evenly coat.

3. Spoon 2 tbsp (30 mL) of the chicken mixture into each of 12 lettuce leaves. Serve immediately.

SERVING SIZE: 2 lettuce cups

TOBY'S TIPS: Lighten up this recipe by using light mayonnaise and nonfat plain Greek yogurt.

•

Swap the canned oranges for fresh clementine or mandarin oranges. Peel off the outer casing of each fruit segment and slice into thirds before using.

CHICKEN AVOCADO TOAST

Avocado toast has become quite a sensation. You can find signature takes on it at cafés and restaurant brunches, and it's simple to make at home or for a breaktime snack. Adding chicken to your avo toast ups the protein, and while any bread will do, whole wheat makes this favorite dish even more satisfying.

1 ripe avocado, halved and pitted

2 slices 100% whole wheat bread, toasted

¼ cup (60 mL) finely chopped rotisserie chicken

4 cherry tomatoes, halved

2 tsp (10 mL) chopped fresh cilantro

¼ tsp (1 mL) Thai chile sauce (such as Sriracha)

⅛ tsp (0.5 mL) salt

2 lime wedges

1. Scoop out the flash from each avocado half onto a slice of toasted bread. Mash the avocado with a fork until it is flattened.

2. Top each slice of bread with half of the chicken, 4 tomato slices, half of the cilantro, Thai chile sauce and salt. Spritz a lime wedge over the toast immediately before serving.

SERVING SIZE: 1 avocado toast

TOBY'S TIP: Choose avocados that are firm but yield to gentle pressure. They should be heavy for their size without blemishes. Unripened avocados can be placed in a paper bag for 2 to 4 days and then kept in the refrigerator for several days. To speed up the ripening process, place the avocado in a paper bag with an apple or a banana.

EASY CHICKEN ZUCCHINI BOATS

Zucchini boats are a fun appetizer that tends to stimulate lots of conversation. Once you get the hang of how to make the boats, you can fill them with anything you'd like, including the filling for the Southwest Chicken and Rice Stuffed Peppers (page 112) or cook the zucchini boats first and then fill with the Mandarin Chicken Lettuce Cups (page 50).

PREHEAT THE OVEN TO 350°F (180°C)

Nonstick cooking spray

6 zucchini, halved lengthwise

2 cups (500 mL) chopped rotisserie chicken

1 cup (250 mL) store-bought marinara sauce

¾ cup (175 mL) shredded mozzarella cheese

Thai chile sauce (such as Sriracha, optional)

1. Coat a baking dish with nonstick cooking spray.

2. Using a teaspoon, scoop out the seeds of the zucchini halves and discard. Arrange the zucchini halves in the prepared baking dish, leaving space between each zucchini.

3. Add the chicken and tomato sauce to a medium sauté pan and cook over medium heat, stirring occasionally, until the chicken is warmed through, 5 minutes. Set aside and let cool slightly.

4. Spoon the chicken mixture evenly into each of the zucchini boats and top each boat with 1 tbsp (15 mL) of the cheese. Drizzle with Thai chile sauce (if using). Bake in the preheated oven until the zucchini are tender and the cheese has melted, 20 minutes.

SERVING SIZE: 1 boat

TOBY'S TIPS: Lighten up this appetizer by using shredded part-skim mozzarella cheese.

•

When selecting zucchini, size matters! Larger zucchini tend to be less flavorful and more watery with larger seeds. Look for smaller zucchini, around 8 inches (20 cm) long. Store in a paper bag in the refrigerator for up to 1 week. Avoid storing in plastic bags, which can make the zucchini slimy.

CHICKEN AND CHEESE TORTILLA PIZZA

There's no reason to fuss with pizza dough when you can easily use tortillas as your crust. To dress up this recipe, finely chop your favorite vegetables (like broccoli, mushrooms or bell peppers) and sprinkle over the top.

PREHEAT THE OVEN TO 400°F (200°C)

Nonstick cooking spray

Four 8-inch (20 cm) flour tortillas

1 cup (250 mL) store-bought marinara sauce

1 cup (250 mL) finely chopped rotisserie chicken

2 cups (500 mL) shredded mozzarella cheese

1. Coat two baking sheets with nonstick cooking spray.

2. Place 2 tortillas on each of the prepared baking sheets. Top each tortilla with ¼ cup (60 mL) of the tomato sauce, using the back of a spoon to spread it evenly over the tortilla. Next, sprinkle each tortilla with ¼ cup (60 mL) of the chicken and top with ½ cup (125 mL) of the cheese.

3. Place the baking sheets in the preheated oven and bake until the cheese is bubbling and the tortillas are slightly browned, 8 to 10 minutes. Remove the baking sheets from the oven and allow the pizzas to rest for about 5 minutes before slicing each pizza into 4 quarters.

SERVING SIZE: 2 wedges

TOBY'S TIPS: Lighten up this recipe by using part-skim shredded mozzarella cheese. Use whole wheat tortillas to increase the fiber.

•

When buying marinara sauce, there are many options available. Watch for brands that add sugar. Compare labels and select the brand with the least amount of added sugar.

CHICKEN CROQUETTES

Instead of fussing with ground chicken for croquettes, your precooked rotisserie chicken can save you time. In this recipe, all of the ingredients are tossed into a blender to make the batter, which you form into croquettes and cook. It can't get much easier to create a delicious appetizer that everyone will love.

BLENDER

4 cups (1 L) finely chopped rotisserie chicken

½ cup (125 mL) panko bread crumbs

1 yellow onion, chopped

1 stalk celery, chopped

1 large egg, beaten

1 tsp (5 mL) dried parsley

½ tsp (2 mL) salt

¼ tsp (1 mL) freshly ground black pepper

¼ cup (60 mL) olive oil or canola oil

Spicy mustard, for serving

1. Place the chicken, bread crumbs, onion, celery, egg, parsley, salt and pepper in a blender and pulse until combined and the mixture is slightly chunky, about 30 seconds.

2. Spoon out 1 heaping tbsp (15 mL) of the chicken mixture, and using clean hands, form into a patty. Place it on a large plate or a platter, gently pressing down with the palm of your hand to flatten it slightly. Repeat to make a total of 30 small patties. Cover the platter with plastic wrap and refrigerate for at least 20 minutes or up to 1 hour.

3. In a large sauté pan, heat the oil over medium heat. When the oil is shimmering, add half the croquettes, leaving around 1 inch (2.5 cm) of space between each. Cover the pan and sauté until golden brown, about 4 minutes per side. Transfer the croquettes to a platter. Cover with foil to keep warm, and repeat with the remaining patties. Serve with the spicy mustard for dipping.

SERVING SIZE: 3 croquettes

TOBY'S TIP: Swap the spicy mustard with Dijon or yellow mustard.

CHAPTER 5

SOUPS AND SANDWICHES

CHICKEN NOODLE SOUP

Instead of buying canned or premade chicken soup, you can easily make your own in about 20 minutes. See Toby's Tip for a time-saving trick.

3 cups (750 mL) egg noodles

1 tbsp (15 mL) olive oil

1 yellow onion, chopped

2 cloves garlic, minced

1 carrot, chopped

1 stalk celery, chopped

2 cups (500 mL) chopped rotisserie chicken

6 cups (1.5 L) reduced-sodium ready-to-use chicken broth

½ tsp (2 mL) dried dillweed

¼ tsp (1 mL) salt

⅛ tsp (0.5 mL) freshly ground black pepper

1. Fill a medium saucepan three-quarters with water and bring to a boil over high heat. Stir in the egg noodles and return the water to a boil. Lower the heat to medium, and boil gently until the noodles are al dente, 5 minutes. Using a colander, drain the noodles and set aside in a medium bowl, covered with foil.

2. In a large pot over medium heat, heat the oil. When the oil is shimmering, add the onion, garlic, carrot and celery, and cook for about 5 minutes, until the onion is translucent and the garlic is fragrant.

3. Add the chicken and stir to combine. Add the broth, dillweed, salt and pepper, and stir together. Increase the heat to high and bring the mixture to a boil. Reduce the heat to medium-low, cover and simmer until the flavors combine, 15 minutes.

4. To serve, divide the noodles evenly into each of four soup bowls. Using a ladle, top the noodles with the soup.

MAKE AHEAD: The egg noodles can be cooked up to 3 days in advance and stored, covered, in the refrigerator.

SERVING SIZE: 1½ cups (375 mL)

TOBY'S TIP: The egg noodles are stored separately because they fall apart when stored in the soup. If you want to store the noodles in the soup, use 1 cup (250 mL) dry elbow macaroni, ditalini or orzo pasta and add it directly to the soup along with the broth, dillweed, salt and pepper.

SIMPLE CASSOULET SOUP

Cassoulet is a French stew that varies based on the availability of ingredients and the town in which it was made. One constant is that it does contain white beans, which were imported to France after Columbus's voyages to the Americas and eventually cultivated extensively throughout southwest France.

1 tbsp (15 mL) olive oil or canola oil

1 yellow onion, chopped

5 oz (150 g) andouille sausage, sliced into 1-inch (2.5 cm) rounds

½ tsp (2 mL) dried thyme

½ tsp (2 mL) dried parsley

½ cup (125 mL) white cooking wine or dry white wine

2½ cups (625 mL) reduced-sodium ready-to-use chicken broth

14- to 19-oz (398 to 540 mL) can reduced-sodium cannellini beans, drained and rinsed

14-oz (398 mL) can diced tomatoes, with juice

2 cups (500 mL) chopped rotisserie chicken

¼ tsp (1 mL) salt

¼ tsp (1 mL) freshly ground black pepper

1. Heat the oil in a large pot over medium heat. When the oil is shimmering, add the onion, sausage, thyme and parsley and stir to combine. Cook until the sausage is slightly browned on both sides, about 8 minutes. Add the cooking wine and raise the heat to high and bring to a boil. Cook, stirring occasionally, until the wine is reduced by half, about 2 minutes. Add the chicken broth, beans, tomatoes with juice, chicken, salt and pepper and bring the mixture to a boil. Reduce the heat to medium-low and simmer, covered, until the flavors combine, 10 minutes.

SERVING SIZE: 1¾ cups (425 mL)

TOBY'S TIPS: To lighten up the cassoulet, use chicken andouille sausage.

The Cajun seasoning in andouille sausage adds heat to this dish, but there are many sausage flavors on the market. If you prefer a milder taste, try a smoked turkey sausage.

MULLIGATAWNY SOUP

This soup originates from South Indian cuisine and literally means "pepper water." It was created by servants for the English Raj (or Crown Rule of India when the British ruled), who demanded a soup course when they had never produced one.

1 tbsp (15 mL) olive oil

1 yellow onion, chopped

2 cloves garlic, minced

1 carrot, chopped

1 stalk celery, chopped

1 tbsp (15 mL) curry powder

4 cups (1 L) reduced-sodium ready-to-use chicken broth

1 apple, peeled, cored and chopped

½ cup (125 mL) long-grain white rice

2 cups (500 mL) diced rotisserie chicken

½ tsp (2 mL) salt

⅛ tsp (0.5 mL) freshly ground black pepper

14-oz (400 mL) can light coconut milk

1. Heat the oil in a large stockpot over medium heat. Add the onion and garlic and cook until the onion is translucent and the garlic is fragrant, 3 minutes. Add the carrot and celery and continue cooking until the vegetables soften, 3 minutes. Add the curry powder and toss with the cooked vegetables; cook for 1 minute, stirring occasionally. Add the chicken broth, apple, rice, chicken, salt and pepper and stir to combine. Raise the heat to high and bring the mixture to a boil. Reduce the heat to medium-low, cover and simmer until the flavors combine and the rice is cooked, 15 to 20 minutes. Stir in the coconut milk and continue cooking until heated through, 5 more minutes.

SERVING SIZE: 1½ cups (375 mL)

TOBY'S TIPS: Mulligatawny soup is traditionally made with white rice, but you can swap the white for brown if you choose and cook it for 40 minutes, or swap for a different whole grain, like farro or barley.

-

I like A Taste of Thai coconut milk.

TOBY'S TIPS: When shopping for kale, choose deeply colored leaves for the best flavor. Avoid dry, wilted and limp leaves or those with tiny holes that may be a sign of insect damage. Store unwashed kale in a plastic bag along with a moist paper towel and place in the refrigerator. Use within 3 days.

- Another substitute for mirin is rice vinegar with ½ tsp (2 mL) sugar per 1 tbsp (15 mL).

HEARTY ROOT VEGETABLE AND CHICKEN SOUP

During the winter there are few vegetables that are in season, especially in areas that get a lot of cold weather and snow. That is the perfect time to turn to delicious root vegetables and create this warming soup filled with good-for-you nutrients.

2 tbsp (30 mL) olive oil or canola oil

1 yellow onion, chopped

1 carrot, chopped

1 stalk celery, chopped

1 turnip, chopped

2 parsnips, chopped

14- to 19-oz (398 to 540 mL) can reduced-sodium cannellini beans, drained and rinsed

2 cups (500 mL) chopped rotisserie chicken

6 cups (1.5 L) reduced-sodium ready-to-use chicken broth

1 tbsp (15 mL) mirin, dry sherry or sweet marsala wine

2 bay leaves

¼ tsp (1 mL) salt

¼ tsp (1 mL) freshly ground black pepper

2 cups (500 mL) packed chopped kale or baby kale

1. Heat the oil in a large pot over medium heat. When the oil is shimmering, add the onion, carrot, celery, turnip and parsnips and sauté until the onion is translucent and the vegetables begin to soften, about 5 minutes. Add the beans and chicken and stir to combine. Add the chicken broth, mirin, bay leaves, salt and pepper and stir to combine. Increase the heat to high and bring the liquid to a boil, then reduce the heat to medium-low, cover the pot and simmer until the flavors combine and the vegetables are cooked, 20 minutes. Stir in the kale and allow to wilt, 2 minutes. Remove and discard the bay leaves before serving.

MAKE AHEAD: To save time on a busy weeknight, chop all your vegetables and dice the rotisserie chicken in the morning before work or the night before. Place the ingredients in a covered container and use within 24 hours.

SERVING SIZE: 2 cups (500 mL)

SIMPLE CHICKEN AND CORN CHOWDER

This warming chowder uses milk instead of heavy or whipping cream, so it is a great choice when you're looking for a hearty dish that doesn't require a post-lunch nap. Adding chicken to corn chowder ups the protein, making this filling chowder a balanced meal in a bowl.

BLENDER

1 tbsp (15 mL) olive oil or canola oil

1 yellow onion, chopped

1 clove garlic, minced

1 stalk celery, chopped

1 red bell pepper, chopped

1 jalapeño pepper, seeded and chopped

2 cups (500 mL) reduced-sodium ready-to-use chicken broth

1½ cups (375 mL) frozen corn kernels

¼ tsp (1 mL) dried thyme

¼ + ⅛ tsp (1.5 mL) salt

⅛ tsp (0.5 mL) hot pepper flakes

2 tbsp (30 mL) cornstarch

2 cups (500 mL) 2% milk

2 cups (500 mL) chopped rotisserie chicken

1. Heat the oil in a large stockpot over medium heat. When the oil is shimmering, add the onion and garlic and cook, stirring occasionally, until the onion is translucent, 3 minutes. Add the celery, red pepper and jalapeño and continue cooking until the vegetables have softened slightly, 5 minutes. Add the chicken broth, corn, thyme, salt and pepper flakes and bring to a boil. Reduce the heat to medium-low and simmer, stirring occasionally, until the corn is cooked, about 3 minutes.

2. In a small bowl, whisk together the cornstarch and milk. Slowly add 4 to 5 tbsp (60 to 75 mL) of the soup to the milk mixture to warm it up. Slowly add the milk mixture to the soup, whisking continuously, until the milk is incorporated. Stir in the chicken. Raise the heat to high and bring the mixture to a boil; lower the heat and simmer until the flavors combine, 15 minutes, stirring occasionally.

3. Carefully ladle half the soup into a blender and blend until smooth. Return the blended soup to the stockpot and stir to combine.

SERVING SIZE: 1¼ cups (300 mL)

TOBY'S TIP: Not only does using milk instead of cream make this soup lighter, but you are also more likely to have it on hand! If you like a creamier soup, blend the entire soup instead of only half.

CHICKEN-ALMOND SOUP

This broth-based soup uses both almond butter and toasted almonds to impart a subtle earthy flavor. It's quite delicious and satisfying as a snack or starter.

½ cup (125 mL) slivered almonds

4 cups (1 L) reduced-sodium ready-to-use chicken broth

¼ cup (60 mL) almond butter

1 tbsp (15 mL) olive oil or canola oil

1 leek (white and light green parts only), chopped

2 tbsp (30 mL) unsalted butter

¼ cup (60 mL) all-purpose flour

2 cups (500 mL) chopped rotisserie chicken

1 cup (250 mL) frozen peas

1 tsp (5 mL) unseasoned rice vinegar

1 tsp (5 mL) dried tarragon

½ tsp (2 mL) dried thyme

½ tsp (2 mL) salt

⅛ tsp (0.5 mL) freshly ground black pepper

1. Heat the almonds in a small skillet over medium-low heat until slightly toasted, 3 minutes. Set the skillet aside and let cool slightly.

2. In a medium bowl, whisk together the chicken broth and almond butter until incorporated.

3. Heat the oil in a large stockpot over medium heat. When the oil is shimmering, add the leek and cook, stirring occasionally, until slightly softened, 3 minutes. Add the butter and allow to melt, stirring to incorporate. Sprinkle the mixture with the flour and stir for about 1 minute. Slowly add the chicken broth mixture while continuously whisking to avoid any clumping. Add the toasted almonds, chicken, peas, rice vinegar, tarragon, thyme, salt and pepper and bring the mixture to a boil, whisking regularly. Reduce the heat and simmer, uncovered, until the flavors combine and the soup thickens, 12 minutes.

MAKE AHEAD: Toast the almonds up to a week in advance. Store in a sealable container in a cool, dry place.

SERVING SIZE: 1⅓ cups (325 mL)

TOBY'S TIP: To clean leeks, trim the root end and remove the dark green tops. Halve lengthwise and then thinly slice into half-moons. Submerge in a bowl filled with cold water to remove grit.

CHICKEN QUINOA SOUP

Quinoa, which is technically a seed, is one of my favorite powerhouse ingredients to add to soups. It has a healthy dose of both fiber and protein, which makes this soup quite hearty. It's also really easy to incorporate — just add quinoa 15 minutes before the soup is done cooking.

1 tbsp (15 mL) olive oil or canola oil

1 yellow onion, chopped

1 clove garlic, minced

2 carrots, sliced into 1-inch (2.5 cm) rounds

2 stalks celery, cut diagonally into 1-inch (2.5 cm) slices

6 cups (1.5 L) reduced-sodium ready-to-use chicken broth

2 cups (500 mL) shredded rotisserie chicken

⅓ cup (75 mL) quinoa

2 bay leaves

½ tsp (2 mL) dried thyme

½ tsp (2 mL) salt

¼ tsp (1 mL) freshly ground black pepper

4 cups (1 L) packed baby spinach, cut into ribbons

1. Heat the oil in a large stockpot over medium heat. When the oil is shimmering, add the onion and garlic and cook, stirring occasionally, until the onion is translucent and the garlic is fragrant, 3 minutes. Add the carrots and celery and cook, stirring occasionally, until the vegetables are slightly softened, 5 minutes. Add the chicken broth, chicken, quinoa, bay leaves, thyme, salt and pepper and raise the heat to high and bring the mixture to a boil. Then lower the heat and simmer until the flavors combine and the quinoa is cooked through, 15 minutes. Stir in the spinach and cook until wilted, 2 minutes.

SERVING SIZE: 1¾ cups (425 mL)

TOBY'S TIP: Swap the chicken broth with reduced-sodium vegetable broth or use a combination of both.

MEXICAN CHICKEN SOUP

This tasty soup combines your favorite Mexican-inspired flavors in one bowl of goodness. Who could ask for more? If you want more of a kick, see Toby's Tips for ideas on increasing the heat.

1 tbsp (15 mL) olive oil or canola oil

1 yellow onion, chopped

1 stalk celery, chopped

1 red bell pepper, chopped

4 cups (1 L) reduced-sodium ready-to-use chicken broth

28-oz (796 mL) can reduced-sodium diced tomatoes, with juice

14- to 19-oz (398 to 540 mL) can reduced-sodium black beans, drained and rinsed

2 cups (500 mL) chopped rotisserie chicken

4½-oz (127 mL) can diced green chiles, with juice

1 tsp (5 mL) garlic powder

1 tsp (5 mL) ground cumin

1 tsp (5 mL) ground coriander

1 tsp (5 mL) freshly squeezed lime juice

½ tsp (2 mL) salt

¼ tsp (1 mL) freshly ground black pepper

TOPPINGS (OPTIONAL)

Tortilla chips

Sour cream or plain Greek yogurt

1. Heat the oil in a large stockpot over medium heat. When the oil is shimmering, add the onion, celery and red pepper and cook, stirring occasionally, until the onion is translucent, 3 minutes. Add the chicken broth, tomatoes with juice, black beans, chicken, green chiles with juice, garlic powder, cumin, coriander, lime juice, salt and pepper. Raise the heat to high and bring the mixture to a boil, and then lower the heat and simmer until the flavors combine, 15 minutes. Serve with tortilla chips and sour cream (if using).

SERVING SIZE: 1⅔ cups (400 mL)

TOBY'S TIPS: Lighten up the toppings by using reduced-fat sour cream or reduced-fat plain Greek yogurt.

To add heat, use "hot" diced green chiles or add a diced jalapeño to the soup. You can also serve the soup with hot pepper sauce so individuals can customize their heat level.

EASY CHICKEN WRAP

A quick and easy go-to lunch is a chicken wrap. If you need to save 5 minutes, skip the diced vegetables and just add a few lettuce leaves and tomato slices.

2 kirby or Persian cucumbers, diced

2 plum (Roma) tomatoes, diced

1 avocado, diced

$\frac{1}{4}$ red onion, chopped

Juice of 1 lemon

2 tbsp (30 mL) extra virgin olive oil

$\frac{1}{4}$ tsp (1 mL) salt

$\frac{1}{8}$ tsp (0.5 mL) freshly ground black pepper

Nonstick cooking spray

Four 8-inch (20 cm) flour tortillas

2 cups (500 mL) chopped rotisserie chicken (cold or warm)

1 cup (250 mL) shredded mozzarella cheese

1. In a medium bowl, toss together the cucumbers, tomatoes, avocado and red onion. Add the lemon juice, oil, salt and pepper and toss to combine.

2. Coat a medium skillet with nonstick cooking spray and place over medium-low heat. Add a tortilla and cook for 30 seconds on each side until warmed through. Place the heated tortilla on a clean plate and cover with a paper towel to keep warm. Repeat with the remaining tortillas.

3. Place a warmed tortilla on a separate large plate. Spoon $\frac{1}{4}$ cup (60 mL) of the vegetables onto the tortilla, then top with $\frac{1}{2}$ cup (125 mL) of the chicken and $\frac{1}{4}$ cup (60 mL) of the cheese. Fold the bottom edge of each tortilla up and over the filling, fold in the opposite sides and roll up from the bottom. Repeat for a total of 4 wraps.

MAKE AHEAD: The salad can be made up to 24 hours in advance.

SERVING SIZE: 1 wrap

TOBY'S TIPS: Lighten up this recipe by using shredded part-skim mozzarella cheese. Make it more filling by using whole wheat tortillas.

•

To check if an avocado is ripe, hold it in the palm of your hand and gently give it a squeeze. A ripe avocado should yield to firm, gentle pressure. If it's too firm, place it in a paper bag with an apple, which will speed up ripening.

GRILLED APPLE, GOUDA AND CHICKEN PANINI

Gouda pairs beautifully with the sweet flavor of apples in this warm sandwich. Don't have a panini press? Not to worry! See the method for instructions on using a grill pan or skillet to make this sandwich.

GRILL PAN

¼ cup (60 mL) mayonnaise, divided

4 ciabatta rolls, sliced open

8 tsp (40 mL) Dijon mustard, divided

1 Granny Smith apple, thinly sliced into half-moons

1 cup (250 mL) shredded rotisserie chicken, divided

4 oz (100 g) smoked Gouda cheese, cut into 4 even slices

Nonstick cooking spray

1. Spread 1 tbsp (15 mL) mayonnaise on one half of a ciabatta roll and 2 tsp (10 mL) Dijon mustard on the other half of the ciabatta roll. Repeat for the remaining rolls.

2. Layer the bottom halves with 2 or 3 apple slices, ¼ cup (60 mL) rotisserie chicken and 1 slice Gouda cheese. Place the top of the roll over the cheese to close the sandwich.

3. Coat a grill pan or skillet with nonstick cooking spray and place over medium heat. When the pan is hot, add one panini and use a second skillet to gently press down. Cook until the bread is slightly toasted and the cheese has started to melt, 3 minutes on each side. Slice the sandwich in half before serving.

MAKE AHEAD: These panini can be made in advance for meal prepping. Store the uncooked panini in the refrigerator for up to 3 days and cook right before eating.

SERVING SIZE: 1 panino

TOBY'S TIPS: Lighten up this recipe by using light mayonnaise.

Get a little creative with your panini by switching up the cheese and fruit. Gouda is sold as smoked or regular, and try swapping the apple for pear.

CHICKEN SHAWARMA STUFFED PITA

Shawarma is a Middle Eastern dish that is created when meat is roasted, specifically on a revolving stick or spit, then shaved and served in sandwiches. Although you're skipping the time-consuming step of cooking the meat, those fragrant spices will infuse mouthwatering flavor into your homemade shawarma-style stuffed pita.

2 tbsp (30 mL) olive oil

Juice of ½ lemon

½ tsp (1 mL) ground coriander

½ tsp (1 mL) ground cumin

¼ tsp (1 mL) ground ginger

¼ tsp (1 mL) salt

⅛ tsp (0.5 mL) freshly ground black pepper

⅛ tsp (0.5 mL) turmeric

⅛ tsp (0.5 mL) allspice

⅛ tsp (0.5 mL) ground cinnamon

3 cups (750 mL) shredded rotisserie chicken

Four 8-inch (20 cm) pitas

8 leaves lettuce, sliced in half widthwise

1 cup (250 mL) Tzatziki Sauce (page 179) or store-bought tzatziki

1. In a medium bowl, whisk together the oil, lemon juice, coriander, cumin, ginger, salt, pepper, turmeric, allspice and cinnamon. Add the chicken and toss to combine.

2. Heat a medium skillet over medium heat. When the skillet is hot, add the chicken mixture and cook until the chicken is heated through, 6 to 8 minutes.

3. Use a knife to cut 1 inch (2.5 cm) from the top of the pita. Open the slit and insert 2 slices of lettuce, spoon in ¾ cup (175 mL) of the chicken mixture and top with ¼ cup (60 mL) of the tzatziki. Repeat for a total of 4 sandwiches.

MAKE AHEAD: The Tzatziki Sauce can be made up to 3 days in advance.

SERVING SIZE: 1 pita

TOBY'S TIPS: Give this dish a nutritional boost by using whole wheat pita.

Ground spices can be stored for 2 to 3 years in a cool, dark place — like your pantry! If you've been stashing your ground spices longer than that, it's time to invest in new ones.

BBQ CHICKEN SLIDERS

This family favorite dish will quickly become one of the most requested in your home. If you don't have time to make the Homemade Barbecue Sauce, choose a store-bought barbecue sauce with less added sugar — just compare labels — and stash one or two extra bottles in your pantry.

1 tbsp (15 mL) olive oil

1 shallot, chopped

1 clove garlic, minced

4 cups (1 L) shredded rotisserie chicken

¾ cup (175 mL) Homemade Barbecue Sauce (page 178) or store-bought barbecue sauce

12 slider buns

12 slices sharp (old) Cheddar cheese

3 plum (Roma) tomatoes, thinly sliced

12 leaves romaine, sliced in half widthwise

1. Heat the oil in a medium skillet over medium heat. When the oil is shimmering, add the shallot and garlic and cook until the shallot softens and the garlic is fragrant, 2 minutes. Add the rotisserie chicken and barbecue sauce and toss to combine. Reduce the heat to medium-low and continue cooking until the flavors combine and the chicken is heated through, 5 minutes.

2. On each of 12 slider buns, place 1 slice of cheese and top with ¼ cup (60 mL) of the warm barbecue chicken mixture. Next, top with a few tomato slices and 2 lettuce leaf halves. Serve warm.

SERVING SIZE: 2 sliders

TOBY'S TIPS: Lighten up this recipe by using reduced-fat Cheddar cheese, and make it more filling by using whole wheat slider buns.

•

Storing tomatoes in the refrigerator makes them dull and mealy. For the tastiest tomatoes, store them on the countertop at room temperature.

MAKES 5 SERVINGS

CURRIED CHICKEN AND PEAR SALAD WRAP

Shake up your everyday chicken salad by adding a little curry and balancing it with the sweetness of raisins and pears, and the crunchiness of almonds.

⅓ cup (75 mL) mayonnaise

¼ cup (60 mL) plain Greek yogurt

2 tsp (10 mL) freshly squeezed lemon juice

1 tsp (5 mL) brown sugar

½ tsp (2 mL) curry powder

⅛ tsp (0.5 mL) salt

⅛ tsp (0.5 mL) freshly ground black pepper

3 cups (750 mL) chopped rotisserie chicken

2 green onions, chopped

1 pear, finely diced

½ cup (125 mL) golden seedless raisins

⅓ cup (75 mL) unsalted roasted almonds, finely chopped

Five 8-inch (20 cm) flour tortillas

10 leaves lettuce

1. In a medium bowl, whisk together the mayonnaise, yogurt, lemon juice, brown sugar, curry powder, salt and pepper until well combined.

2. Add the chicken, green onions, pear, raisins and almonds to the mayonnaise mixture and toss to evenly coat.

3. Place a tortilla on a large plate or flat surface (like a cutting board). Layer 2 lettuce leaves in the center of the tortilla and top with 1 cup (250 mL) of the chicken salad. Fold the bottom edge of each tortilla up and over the filling, fold in the opposite sides and roll up from the bottom. Repeat for a total of 5 wraps.

SERVING SIZE: 1 wrap

TOBY'S TIPS: Lighten up this dish by using light mayonnaise and nonfat plain Greek yogurt, and give it a nutritional boost by using whole wheat tortillas.

- To check if a pear is ripe, check the neck. Gently apply pressure around the neck of the pear with your thumb and forefinger. If the fruit yields to the pressure, then you've got yourself a nice, juicy pear. Once a pear is ripe, you can store it in the fridge for up to 5 days.

Experiment with different cheeses. Cheddar is a melt standard and comes in mild to extra-sharp flavors. You can also use the following cheeses, which all melt beautifully:

- **COLBY:** This orange cheese is a similar color to Cheddar and can be used anywhere Cheddar is used.

- **PROVOLONE:** This Italian cheese has a milder flavor and works well with bold flavors.

- **MONTEREY JACK:** This whitish cheese melts beautifully between two slices of bread. To add heat, opt for hot pepper Jack cheese (jalapeños are added to the cheese).

- **BLUE CHEESE:** This tangy, bold cheese complements sweet flavors.

BASIC CHICKEN MELT

This chicken melt is quick to make and easy to clean up after cooking. It's perfect for lunch or dinner. The recipe calls for Cheddar, but see the opposite page for other cheeses that also melt well.

Nonstick cooking spray

4 slices bread

8 slices Cheddar cheese

1 cup (250 mL) coarsely chopped rotisserie chicken

1 plum (Roma) tomato, thinly sliced

1 green onion, chopped (whites and greens)

1. Coat a medium skillet with nonstick cooking spray and heat over medium heat. Add 1 slice of bread and cook until slightly toasted, 1 minute. Top with 1 slice of cheese, ¼ cup (60 mL) of the chicken, 1 to 2 slices of tomato, one-fourth of the green onion, a second slice of cheese and then top with a second slice of bread. Continue cooking until the cheese has slightly melted, 2 to 3 minutes.

2. Gently flip the sandwich, holding the top as you turn it over. Cook until the bread is toasted and the cheese is melty, 3 to 4 minutes more. Repeat with the remaining sandwiches.

SERVING SIZE: 1 melt

TOBY'S TIPS: Using 100% whole wheat, whole rye or your other favorite whole-grain bread will help you get your daily fill of the fiber and nutrients found in whole grains, like protein, B vitamins, antioxidants, iron, zinc, copper and magnesium. Whole grains are beneficial because they can help keep your gastrointestinal tract healthy, and help reduce the risk of heart disease, type 2 diabetes and some forms of cancer.

·

Lighten up this recipe by using reduced-fat Cheddar cheese.

CHICKEN CLUB WRAP

Haas avocados work well in sandwiches, salads and wraps like this one. One ounce (28 g) of a Haas avocado provides twenty vitamins and minerals, as well as phytonutrients (plant chemicals that help fight and prevent disease), including lutein and zeaxanthin, which has been shown to help maintain healthy eyes as you age.

Nonstick cooking spray

4 slices (1 oz/30 g each slice) uncured bacon

¼ cup (60 mL) mayonnaise

2 tbsp (30 mL) plain Greek yogurt

1 tsp (5 mL) cider vinegar

¼ tsp (1 mL) salt

⅛ tsp (0.5 mL) freshly ground black pepper

2 cups (500 mL) shredded rotisserie chicken

Four 8-inch (20 cm) flour tortillas

2 cups (500 mL) shredded lettuce

1 plum (Roma) tomato, thinly sliced

½ Haas avocado, thinly sliced

1. Coat a large skillet with nonstick cooking spray and heat over medium heat. When the oil is shimmering, add the bacon and cook until browned and crisp, about 3 minutes on each side. Remove the bacon from the skillet and place on a paper towel to drain excess fat.

2. In a medium bowl, whisk together the mayonnaise, Greek yogurt, vinegar, salt and pepper. Add the chicken and toss to evenly coat.

3. Place 1 tortilla on a large plate or flat surface (like a cutting board). Sprinkle ¼ cup (60 mL) of the shredded lettuce along the center of the tortilla and top with several slices of the tomato and avocado. Crumble 1 slice of bacon over the top and add ½ cup (125 mL) of the chicken mixture. Fold the bottom edge of each tortilla up and over the filling, fold in the opposite sides and roll up from the bottom. Repeat for a total of 4 wraps.

SERVING SIZE: 1 wrap

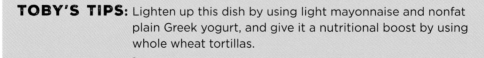

TOBY'S TIPS: Lighten up this dish by using light mayonnaise and nonfat plain Greek yogurt, and give it a nutritional boost by using whole wheat tortillas.

- When choosing bacon, I like Applegate Naturals bacon.

CAJUN CHICKEN MELT

If you like to add spice to your meals, keep a container of Cajun seasoning in your spice drawer. You can find Cajun seasoning at local supermarkets or online grocers. It's an all-in-one spice that you can use on vegetables, like potatoes; grain dishes; or in the mayo mixture in this sandwich.

1 cup (250 mL) chopped rotisserie chicken

1 shallot finely chopped

1 stalk celery, chopped

1 carrot, shredded

¼ cup (60 mL) mayonnaise

¼ cup (60 mL) plain Greek yogurt

½ tsp (1 mL) Cajun seasoning

Nonstick cooking spray

8 slices bread

8 slices Cheddar cheese

1. In a medium bowl, mix together the chicken, shallot, celery and carrot. Add the mayonnaise, yogurt and Cajun seasoning and toss to evenly combine.

2. Coat a medium skillet with nonstick cooking spray and heat over medium heat. Add 1 slice of bread and cook until slightly toasted, 1 minute. Top the bread with 1 slice of cheese, ⅓ cup (70 mL) of the chicken mixture, another slice of cheese and top with a second slice of bread. Continue cooking until the cheese has slightly melted, 2 to 3 minutes.

3. Gently flip the sandwich, holding the top as you turn it over. Cook until the bread is toasted and the cheese is melty, 3 to 4 minutes. Repeat with the remaining sandwiches.

SERVING SIZE: 1 melt

TOBY'S TIPS: Lighten up this dish by using light mayonnaise, nonfat plain Greek yogurt and reduced-fat Cheddar cheese. To add more nutrition to your bread, opt for whole grains like 100% whole wheat or seedless rye bread.

- To add even more spice, up the Cajun seasoning to ¾ tsp (1.5 mL) and swap the Cheddar for pepper Jack cheese.

CHIPOTLE CHICKEN GRILLED CHEESE

Cilantro is an herb that some people absolutely love and others say tastes like soap. Genetics determine which taste profile you'll have — so unless you give it a try, you'll never know. Of course, you can always add more cilantro to this sandwich, or you could skip it if it's not a favorite in your home.

2 canned chipotle peppers in adobo sauce, divided, plus 1 tbsp (15 mL) adobo sauce

¼ cup (60 mL) mayonnaise

1 cup (250 mL) chopped rotisserie chicken

2 tbsp (30 mL) chopped fresh cilantro

4 English muffins, split in halves

Nonstick cooking spray

8 slices mozzarella cheese

1. Finely chop 1 chipotle pepper and place it in a small bowl. Add the mayonnaise and stir until well combined.

2. Finely chop the second chipotle pepper. In a medium bowl, add the chopped chipotle pepper, chicken, cilantro and adobo sauce.

3. Spread the chipotle mayonnaise evenly among the 8 English muffin halves.

4. Coat a skillet with nonstick cooking spray and heat over medium heat. When the oil is shimmering, place the dry side of 4 English muffin halves onto the skillet and toast for 1 minute. Top with 1 slice of cheese, ¼ cup (60 mL) of the chicken mixture, a second slice of cheese and then the second half of the English muffin. Continue cooking until the cheese is slightly melted, 2 to 3 minutes.

5. Gently flip the sandwich, holding the top as you turn it over. Cook until the English muffin is toasted and the cheese is melty, 3 to 4 minutes more.

SERVING SIZE: 1 sandwich

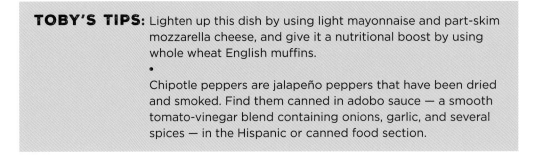

TOBY'S TIPS: Lighten up this dish by using light mayonnaise and part-skim mozzarella cheese, and give it a nutritional boost by using whole wheat English muffins.

• Chipotle peppers are jalapeño peppers that have been dried and smoked. Find them canned in adobo sauce — a smooth tomato-vinegar blend containing onions, garlic, and several spices — in the Hispanic or canned food section.

CHICKEN RANCH WRAP

Everything tastes better with ranch dressing! You can buy bottled dressing from the store or lighten it up by making a batch of Easy Ranch Dressing.

2 cups (500 mL) shredded rotisserie chicken

½ cup (125 mL) Easy Ranch Dressing (page 174) or store-bought ranch dressing

Four 8-inch (20 cm) tortillas

1 cup (250 mL) shredded romaine lettuce

1 plum (Roma) tomato, sliced

1. In a medium bowl, toss together the chicken and ranch dressing.

2. Place a tortilla on a large plate or flat surface (like a cutting board). Place ¼ cup (60 mL) of the shredded lettuce along the center of the tortilla, then top with 1 or 2 slices of tomato and ½ cup (125 mL) of the chicken mixture. Fold the bottom edge of each tortilla up and over the filling, fold in the opposite sides and roll up from the bottom. Repeat for a total of 4 wraps.

SERVING SIZE: 1 wrap

> **TOBY'S TIPS:** If you are using store-bought ranch dressing, lighten this wrap up by using a light ranch dressing, and give it a nutritional boost by using whole wheat tortillas.
>
> • Swap the romaine with baby spinach or shredded kale.

CHICKEN CAPRESE SALAD

One of my favorite flavor combinations is mozzarella, tomato and basil. I enjoy it in salads, adore it in sandwiches and will almost always order any dish that combines this trio when I am out to eat. This version is a simple salad using easy-to-find ingredients that you can whip up in a flash. I like meal prepping it on a Sunday night so I can enjoy it for the next several days when my workweek gets busy.

6 cups (1.5 L) spring mix

1 cup (250 mL) fresh mozzarella balls, halved (see Toby's Tip)

1 cup (250 mL) cherry tomatoes, halved

1½ cups (375 mL) chopped rotisserie chicken

½ cup (250 mL) Simple Balsamic Vinaigrette (page 172)

2 tbsp (30 mL) chopped basil

1. In a large serving bowl, add the spring mix and top with the mozzarella, tomatoes and chicken. Top with the vinaigrette and toss to combine. Garnish with the basil.

MAKE AHEAD: To avoid a mushy salad, pack the dressing on the side and dress the salad right before eating.

SERVING SIZE: 1⅔ cups (400 mL)

TOBY'S TIP: The smaller fresh mozzarella balls are easy to use for this salad, but you can also cube 8 oz (230 g) of fresh mozzarella.

BUFFALO CHICKEN SALAD

I can eat Buffalo-style chicken almost every night of the week. I especially love it in wraps and quesadillas, but I'm always looking for ways to get more vegetables into my day. The answer: this Buffalo Chicken Salad. I get the spiciness I crave from the Buffalo chicken with the crunchiness from the vegetables I love.

2 cups (500 mL) shredded rotisserie chicken

¼ cup (60 mL) Buffalo-style hot pepper sauce

6 cups (1.5 L) romaine lettuce

2 stalks celery, thinly sliced

2 carrots, shredded

½ cup (125 mL) Easy Ranch Dressing (page 174) or store-bought ranch dressing

¼ cup (60 mL) crumbled blue cheese

1. Heat a medium sauté pan over medium heat. Add the chicken and hot sauce and toss to evenly coat the chicken. Continue cooking until the chicken is heated through, about 3 minutes. Set aside to slightly cool.

2. In a large salad bowl, add the lettuce, chicken, celery and carrots. Add the ranch dressing and toss to evenly coat. Sprinkle with the blue cheese.

SERVING SIZE: 2⅓ cups (575 mL)

> **TOBY'S TIPS:** My favorite hot pepper sauce for this dish is Frank's RedHot Sauce.
>
> •
>
> Try this salad with Blue Cheese Dressing (page 170). If you are buying the salad dressing, lighten up the recipe by choosing a reduced-fat ranch or blue cheese dressing.

CHICKEN CAESAR SALAD

You don't need to head to a restaurant to get a crisp, fresh Caesar salad. You can easily make your own at home — with the dressing and croutons, too! Using rotisserie chicken means this salad is ready as soon as the croutons come out of the oven.

PREHEAT THE OVEN TO 350°F (180°C)

CROUTONS

3 tbsp (45 mL) olive oil

1 tsp (5 mL) dried thyme

1 tsp (5 mL) dried rosemary

½ tsp (2 mL) garlic powder

¼ tsp (1 mL) salt

⅛ tsp (0.5 mL) freshly ground black pepper

3 slices bread, cut into ¾-inch (2 cm) squares

SALAD

8 cups (2 L) romaine lettuce, roughly chopped

2 cups (500 mL) chopped rotisserie chicken

¼ cup (60 mL) freshly grated Parmesan cheese

½ cup (125 mL) Easy Caesar Dressing (page 176) or store-bought Caesar dressing

1. **CROUTONS:** In a medium bowl, whisk together the oil, thyme, rosemary, garlic powder, salt and pepper. Add the sliced bread and toss to combine.

2. Spoon the bread into a single layer on a baking sheet and bake in the preheated oven until the croutons are slightly browned, 15 minutes. Set aside to cool.

3. **SALAD:** In a large serving bowl, add the lettuce, chicken and croutons and then sprinkle with the cheese. Add the dressing and toss to evenly coat.

MAKE AHEAD: To meal prep any salad, store the dressing separately on the side and add it right before eating.

•

The croutons can be made up to 1 week in advance and stored in a covered container in a cool, dry place.

SERVING SIZE: 2¾ cups (675 mL)

TOBY'S TIP: Give the croutons a nutritional boost by using 100% whole wheat bread.

COBB SALAD

If you like protein, this Cobb salad is for you! With protein from chicken, eggs, and bacon, this salad provides plenty of protein to keep you feeling satisfied. If you need an even bigger portion, up the leafy greens and add a few more veggies you have on hand, like cucumbers and bell peppers.

Nonstick cooking spray

3 slices bacon

4 cups (1 L) chopped romaine lettuce

1 endive, roughly chopped

1½ cups (375 mL) chopped rotisserie chicken

2 plum (Roma) tomatoes, diced

2 large hard-cooked eggs, diced

1 avocado, diced

½ cup (125 mL) Blue Cheese Dressing (page 170) or store-bought blue cheese dressing

2 tbsp (30 mL) chopped chives

1. Coat a large skillet with nonstick cooking spray and heat over medium heat. When the oil is shimmering, add the bacon and cook until browned and crisp, about 3 minutes on each side. Remove the bacon from the skillet and place on a paper towel. Let cool. Once cooled, chop the bacon.

2. In a large salad bowl, add the romaine lettuce, endive, chicken, tomatoes, eggs, avocado and cooled bacon. Drizzle the dressing over the salad and toss to evenly coat. Sprinkle with the chives.

MAKE AHEAD: The bacon and hard-cooked eggs can be prepared 24 hours in advance. Store in a covered container in the refrigerator.

SERVING SIZE: 2 cups (500 mL)

TOBY'S TIPS: Lighten up this salad by using uncured turkey bacon (I like Applegate Naturals). There are several options that are healthier than good old bacon, including Canadian bacon, turkey bacon, or soy-based bacon (I like Morningstar Farms). Choose the option that works best for you!

If you use store-bought dressing, make it lighter by choosing a lower calorie blue cheese dressing.

LOADED CHICKEN PASTA SALAD

Pasta salad is a favorite dish, but oftentimes is lacking in protein. Adding rotisserie chicken is a quick way to boost the protein, while loading it with vegetables is a fabulous way to up the fiber and add veggies to your day. Both the protein and the fiber have an added benefit of keeping you satisfied for longer.

¼ cup (60 mL) plain Greek yogurt

¼ cup (60 mL) mayonnaise

1 tsp (5 mL) freshly squeezed lemon juice

¼ tsp (1 mL) onion powder

¼ tsp (1 mL) garlic powder

⅛ tsp (0.5 mL) salt

⅛ tsp (0.5 mL) freshly ground black pepper

8 oz (230 g) dry macaroni pasta

1 cup (250 mL) chopped rotisserie chicken

1 cup (250 mL) reduced-sodium chickpeas, drained and rinsed

1 yellow, orange or red bell pepper, diced

½ English (hothouse) cucumber, diced

½ cup (125 mL) pitted green olives, halved lengthwise

1. In a large bowl, whisk together the yogurt, mayonnaise, lemon juice, onion powder, garlic powder, salt and black pepper.

2. Bring a 3-quart (3 L) saucepan of water to a boil over high heat. Add the pasta and return to a boil, then lower the heat to medium and cook until the pasta is al dente, 7 minutes. Drain and rinse under cool water. Set aside to completely cool, 10 minutes.

3. Place the cooled pasta, chicken, chickpeas, yellow pepper, cucumber and olives in the large bowl with the yogurt-mayonnaise mixture and toss to evenly coat.

MAKE AHEAD: Make the pasta 1 to 2 days ahead of time and store in the refrigerator until the salad is ready to assemble.

SERVING SIZE: 1¼ cups (300 mL)

TOBY'S TIPS: Lighten up this dish by using light mayonnaise and nonfat plain Greek yogurt.

• Give it a nutritional boost by using whole wheat pasta. Not a fan of whole wheat pasta? Look for pasta varieties with at least 3 grams of fiber per serving made with other whole grains or from legumes.

SOBA NOODLE SALAD

Soba noodles are a Japanese noodle made from buckwheat. They are nutritionally similar to 100% whole wheat pasta, but soba noodles are much softer in texture. You can find them in your supermarket in the Asian section, online or in specialty stores, including Asian markets.

6 oz (170 g) soba noodles

4 cups (1 L) bite-size broccoli florets

1 cup (250 mL) frozen shelled edamame

½ English (hothouse) cucumber, diced

½ cup (125 mL) Ginger Dressing (page 175) or store-bought ginger dressing

1 cup (250 mL) chopped rotisserie chicken

3 green onions, thinly sliced

1. Bring a 3-quart (3 L) saucepan of water to a boil over high heat. Add the soba noodles and return to a boil. Reduce the heat and boil gently for 5 minutes, then stir in the broccoli and edamame and return to a boil over high heat. Reduce the heat and boil gently until the soba noodles are cooked and the broccoli and edamame are just cooked, 4 minutes. Drain and rinse the ingredients with cool water. Set aside to cool completely for 10 minutes.

2. Place the noodles, broccoli and edamame in a large bowl. Add the cucumber and the ginger dressing and gently toss to combine. Add the chicken and gently toss again. Top with the green onions. Serve the salad cold or at room temperature.

SERVING SIZE: About 2 cups (500 mL)

TOBY'S TIP: Get creative with your vegetables. Switch up or add vegetables like radishes, shredded carrot, bell peppers or red cabbage.

BRUSSELS SPROUTS SALAD WITH CHICKEN, CRANBERRIES AND PECANS

Brussels sprouts are part of the cruciferous vegetable (or cabbage) family, which includes cabbage, mustard greens, cauliflower and broccoli. The veggies in this group have been shown to help reduce the risk of cancer.

FOOD PROCESSOR, FITTED WITH SHREDDING BLADE, OR BOX GRATER

DRESSING

2 tbsp (30 mL) red wine vinegar

2 tbsp (30 mL) Dijon mustard

1 tbsp (15 mL) honey

½ tsp (1 mL) garlic powder

½ tsp (1 mL) salt

⅛ tsp (0.5 mL) freshly ground black pepper

¼ cup (60 mL) extra virgin olive oil

SALAD

4 cups (1 L) Brussels sprouts, or 6 cups (1.5 L) shredded Brussels sprouts

½ cup (125 mL) dried cranberries

½ cup (125 mL) chopped raw pecans

2 cups (500 mL) shredded rotisserie chicken

1. **DRESSING:** In a small bowl, whisk together the red wine vinegar, Dijon mustard, honey, garlic powder, salt and pepper. While constantly whisking, slowly add the oil until combined.

2. **SALAD:** If shredding the Brussels sprouts, use a food processor with a shredding blade or use a box grater. Place the shredded Brussels sprouts in a large bowl.

3. Add the cranberries, pecans and chicken to the Brussels sprouts; toss to combine. Pour the dressing over the salad and gently toss to evenly coat. Cover and refrigerate for at least 30 minutes and up to 2 hours to allow the flavors to combine.

MAKE AHEAD: The dressing can be made up to 5 days ahead and stored in a covered container in the refrigerator.

SERVING SIZE: 2 cups (500 mL)

TOBY'S TIP: Look for firm, tightly closed, bright green Brussels sprouts.

ASIAN CABBAGE SLAW WITH CHICKEN

Unlike salads made with lettuce and spinach, tougher vegetables like cabbage and carrots hold up nicely for longer in the fridge and are perfect for meal prepping. This salad can be dressed when you prep it and stored in the fridge for several days. The vegetables will stay firm and the flavors will be incorporated beautifully for an even more delicious dish.

DRESSING

3 tbsp (45 mL) unseasoned rice vinegar

2 tsp (10 mL) honey

1 clove garlic, minced

2 tsp (10 mL) reduced-sodium soy sauce

1 tsp (5 mL) toasted sesame oil

¼ tsp (1 mL) salt

3 tbsp (45 mL) extra virgin olive oil

SALAD

6 cups (1.5 L) shredded napa cabbage

1½ cups (375 mL) chopped rotisserie chicken

2 carrots, peeled and shredded

1 red bell pepper, cut into ½-inch (1 cm) strips

¼ cup (60 mL) chopped fresh cilantro

2 green onions, chopped

1. **DRESSING:** In a small bowl, whisk together the rice vinegar, honey, garlic, soy sauce, sesame oil and salt. While continuously whisking, slowly drizzle in the oil until combined.

2. **SALAD:** In a large salad bowl, add the cabbage, chicken, carrots, red pepper and cilantro and toss to combine. Drizzle with the dressing and toss to evenly coat. Sprinkle with the green onions.

MAKE AHEAD: The dressing can be made up to 5 days in advance and stored in a sealable container in the refrigerator.

SERVING SIZE: 2½ cups (625 mL)

TOBY'S TIPS: Store fresh cilantro in the fridge with the stems down in a glass of water (changing the water daily) or gently wrap in a damp paper towel and place in a sealable bag in the refrigerator for up to 7 days.

- As an alternative to honey, use agave syrup, which dissolves beautifully in dressings, sauces and beverages.

CHICKEN, PEACH AND GOAT CHEESE SALAD

When summer finally arrives, so do delicious peaches. This salad is the perfect way to use your prepared rotisserie chicken with seasonal peaches for a delightful warm-weather salad. It's also a visually appealing dish to serve during a barbecue or to bring to a potluck meal.

¼ cup (60 mL) raw walnuts, chopped

4 cups (1 L) baby spinach

2 cups (500 mL) chopped rotisserie chicken

2 peaches, chopped into 1-inch (2.5 cm) pieces

½ cup (125 mL) Simple Balsamic Vinaigrette (page 172) or store-bought balsamic vinaigrette

½ cup (125 mL) crumbled goat cheese

1. Heat the walnuts in a small skillet over medium-low heat. Cook until the walnuts are toasted, 3 minutes. Remove the skillet from the heat and allow to cool.

2. In a large salad bowl, add the baby spinach and top with the chicken and peaches. Drizzle with the balsamic vinaigrette and toss to evenly coat. Sprinkle with the goat cheese.

SERVING SIZE: 2 cups (500 mL)

TOBY'S TIPS: If you are buying the salad dressing, lighten up the recipe by choosing a reduced-fat balsamic vinaigrette.

•

When buying fresh peaches, choose ones that give slightly with a gentle squeeze and are fragrant. Avoid those with bruises or blemishes. Store in a paper bag in the fridge for up to 7 days.

CHICKEN, KALE AND WHITE BEAN SALAD

I always recommend stashing canned beans in your pantry, especially if you anticipate a very busy week. This super-quick salad with only five ingredients, including rotisserie chicken and canned cannellini beans, is so satisfying and it takes 15 minutes to whip up.

¼ cup (60 mL) chopped raw walnuts

4 cups (1 L) baby kale

1½ cups (375 mL) chopped rotisserie chicken

14- to 19-oz (398 to 540 mL) can reduced-sodium cannellini beans, drained and rinsed

½ cup (120 mL) Lemon-Herb Vinaigrette (page 171)

1. Heat the walnuts in a small skillet over medium-low heat. Cook until the walnuts are lightly toasted, about 3 minutes. Remove from the heat and let cool.

2. In a large bowl, add the kale, chicken, beans and walnuts. Drizzle with the Lemon-Herb Vinaigrette and toss to evenly coat.

SERVING SIZE: 1¾ cups (425 mL)

TOBY'S TIP: Add tang to your salad by sprinkling it with ¼ cup (60 mL) dried cranberries or tart cherries.

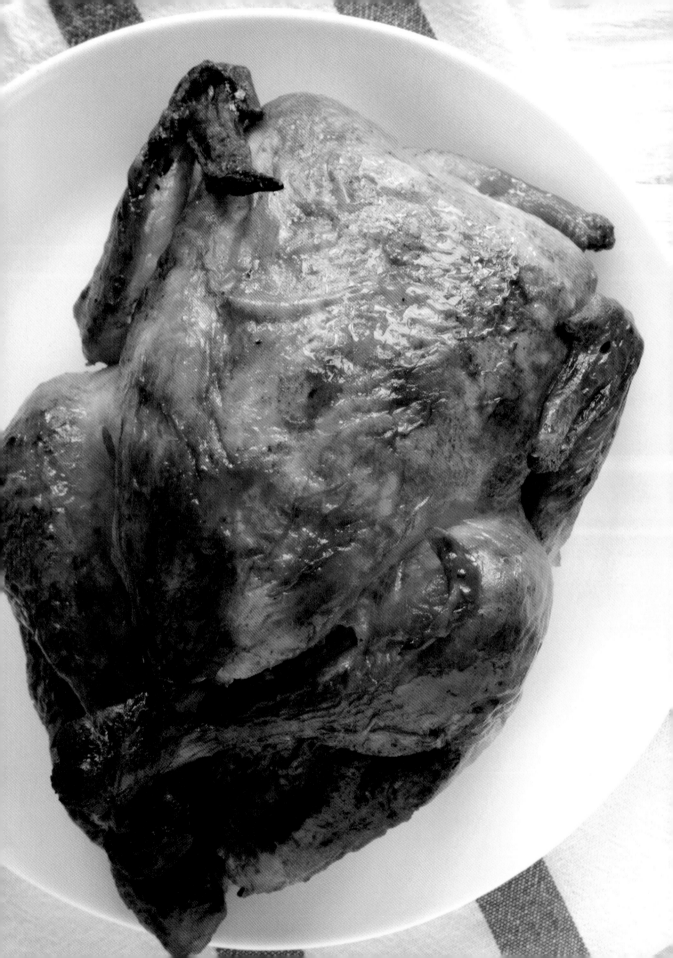

CHAPTER 7

EASY MAINS

CHICKEN AND VEGETABLE STEW

One of the easiest ways to use up extra frozen vegetables is to add them to dishes like this stew. It's also an easy way to help you reach your daily dose of vegetables — adding fresh, frozen or canned varieties can help meet your needs.

1 tbsp (15 mL) olive oil or canola oil

1 yellow onion, chopped

2 cloves garlic, minced

3 tbsp (45 mL) all-purpose flour

1 tsp (5 mL) dried thyme

½ tsp (2 mL) dried basil

3 cups (750 mL) shredded rotisserie chicken

2 cups (500 mL) reduced-sodium ready-to-use chicken broth

2 russet potatoes, diced into 1-inch (2.5 cm) cubes

3 carrots, cut into 1-inch (2.5 cm) rounds

1 red bell pepper, cut into 1-inch (2.5 cm) strips

1 cup (250 mL) frozen peas

¼ cup (60 mL) white cooking wine or dry white wine

3 bay leaves

¼ tsp (1 mL) salt

¼ tsp (1 mL) freshly ground black pepper

1. In a large stockpot, heat the oil over medium heat. When the oil is shimmering, add the onion and garlic and cook, stirring occasionally, until the onion is translucent and the garlic is fragrant, about 2 minutes. Sprinkle in the flour, thyme and basil and stir for 2 minutes. Add the chicken, broth, potatoes, carrots, red pepper, peas, wine, bay leaves, salt and pepper. Raise the heat to high and bring the mixture to a boil. Reduce the heat to medium-low and simmer, covered, for 20 minutes. Remove the bay leaves before serving.

SERVING SIZE: 1½ cups (375 mL)

TOBY'S TIP: To lessen cooking time, use leftover baked russet or sweet potatoes and add as directed in step 1. Reduce the simmer time to 10 minutes, instead of 20 minutes.

CHICKEN PARMESAN CASSEROLE

This dish is a spin on chicken Parmesan. The rotisserie chicken is mixed with penne pasta and lots of delicious Italian spices, tomato sauce and cheese for an outstanding eating experience. Since the chicken isn't breaded and fried, a little sprinkle of bread crumbs on top gives it that extra crunch.

PREHEAT THE OVEN TO 350°F (180°C)

Nonstick cooking spray

8 oz (250 g) penne pasta

2 cups (500 mL) shredded rotisserie chicken

1½ cups (375 mL) tomato sauce, divided

1 tsp (5 mL) dried parsley

1 tsp (5 mL) dried oregano

1 tsp (5 mL) dried basil

¼ tsp (1 mL) salt

⅛ tsp (0.5 mL) freshly ground black pepper

⅛ tsp (0.5 mL) hot pepper flakes

1 cup (250 mL) shredded mozzarella cheese

2 tbsp (30 mL) freshly grated Parmesan cheese

¼ cup (60 mL) Italian-style bread crumbs

1. Coat an 8-inch (20 cm) square glass baking dish with nonstick cooking spray.

2. Bring a 3-quart (3 L) saucepan of water to a boil. Add the penne and boil gently until al dente, 8 to 9 minutes. Drain the pasta and rinse with cool water. Set aside.

3. In a medium bowl, toss together the cooked pasta, chicken, 1 cup (250 mL) of the tomato sauce, parsley, oregano, basil, salt, black pepper and pepper flakes. Spoon the mixture into the prepared baking dish.

4. Top the casserole with the remaining tomato sauce and spread evenly with the back of a spoon. Sprinkle evenly with the mozzarella cheese, Parmesan cheese and bread crumbs. Bake in the preheated oven until the top is bubbly and golden brown, about 25 minutes.

MAKE AHEAD: The penne can be cooked 1 to 2 days in advance and stored, covered, in the refrigerator until ready to incorporate.

SERVING SIZE: 1⅔ cups (400 mL)

TOBY'S TIP: Give this dish a nutritional boost by using whole wheat pasta, and lighten it up by using shredded part-skim cheese.

CHICKEN NOODLE CASSEROLE

Casseroles are a weeknight favorite, but oftentimes are made using heavy cream. Instead, this recipe uses a combination of milk and broth with flour to thicken this filling but lighter casserole. Serve alongside a simple green salad and crusty bread.

PREHEAT THE OVEN TO 350°F (180°C)

Nonstick cooking spray

2 cups (500 mL) wide dry egg noodles (3½ oz/100 g)

2 cups (500 mL) frozen peas and carrots, thawed

1 cup (250 mL) reduced-sodium ready-to-use chicken broth

½ cup (125 mL) milk

½ tsp (2 mL) poultry seasoning

2 tsp (10 mL) olive oil

1 small onion, diced

2 tbsp (30 mL) unsalted butter

6 tbsp (90 mL) unbleached all-purpose flour

1 cup (250 mL) cottage cheese

1½ cups (375 mL) shredded mozzarella cheese

2 cups (500 mL) shredded rotisserie chicken

¼ cup (60 mL) freshly grated Parmesan cheese

1. Coat an 8- by 11-inch (20 by 28 cm) glass baking dish with nonstick cooking spray.

2. Bring a 4-quart (4 L) stockpot of water to a boil over high heat. Stir in the noodles and return to a boil. Reduce the heat and boil gently until the noodles are al dente, 8 minutes. Place the peas and carrots in the bottom of a colander. When the noodles are done, drain over the peas and carrots to warm the vegetables. Set the noodles with vegetables aside to slightly cool.

3. In a microwave-safe small bowl, whisk together the broth, milk and poultry seasoning. Warm the mixture slightly in the microwave on High for 30 seconds. Set aside.

4. In a large saucepan, heat the oil over medium heat. When the oil is shimmering, add the onion and cook, stirring occasionally, until soft and translucent, 3 minutes. Reduce the heat to low and add the butter. When the butter is melted, sprinkle in the flour and cook for 1 minute, whisking constantly. Slowly add the milk mixture while whisking until combined. Continue cooking, stirring occasionally, until the sauce thickens, about 2 minutes. Add the cottage cheese and mozzarella, stir to combine, and then fold in the noodles with the vegetables. Fold in the chicken, then place in the prepared casserole dish and evenly top with the Parmesan cheese.

5. Bake the casserole in the preheated oven until the cheese has melted and the edges are slightly browned, 30 minutes. Remove the casserole from the oven and cool for 10 minutes before serving.

SERVING SIZE: 1 cup (250 mL)

TOBY'S TIPS: Lighten up this casserole even more by using 2% milk, 2% cottage cheese and shredded part-skim mozzarella cheese.

•

In any recipe that calls for reduced-sodium chicken broth, you can use reduced-sodium vegetable broth or water instead. Using water, however, will result in a slightly less flavorful dish, but you can always use it when you're in a pinch.

•

Swap ½ tsp poultry seasoning for ½ tsp dried sage and ¼ tsp dried thyme.

LOADED POTATO CHICKEN CASSEROLE

This fully loaded, cheesy casserole makes a hearty meal on its own. You can cook it and freeze ahead, so it's ready to go during a busy workweek.

PREHEAT THE OVEN TO 400°F (200°C)

Nonstick cooking spray

2 lbs (1 kg) red potatoes, cut into 1-inch (2.5 cm) cubes

2 tbsp (30 mL) olive oil

2 tsp (10 mL) paprika

2 tsp (10 mL) garlic powder

2 tsp (10 mL) hot pepper sauce

¼ tsp (1 mL) salt

⅛ tsp (0.5 mL) freshly ground black pepper

1½ cups (375 mL) shredded rotisserie chicken

1 green bell pepper, diced

1 small red onion, diced

1 jalapeño pepper, seeded and thinly sliced

1 cup (250 mL) shredded Cheddar cheese

TOPPINGS (OPTIONAL)

Sour cream

Chunky Salsa (page 182) or store-bought salsa

1. Coat an 8-inch (20 cm) square glass baking dish with nonstick cooking spray.

2. Pour ½ cup (125 mL) water into a medium pot fitted with a steamer basket, and bring to a boil over high heat. Add the cubed potatoes, cover the pot and lower the heat to medium. Cook the potatoes until tender, 10 minutes. Remove from the pot and let cool for 10 minutes.

3. In a large mixing bowl, whisk together the oil, paprika, garlic powder, hot pepper sauce, salt and black pepper. Add the potatoes and chicken. Toss to evenly coat.

4. Place the potatoes and chicken in the prepared baking dish and use the back of a mixing spoon to even out the top. Spoon the green pepper, red onion and jalapeño evenly over the top, and then sprinkle with the cheese. Bake in the preheated oven until the top is bubbly and the edges are browned, 15 minutes. Serve with sour cream and salsa (if using).

SERVING SIZE: 1⅔ cups (625 mL)

TOBY'S TIPS: Lighten up this dish by using shredded reduced-fat Cheddar cheese and topping with reduced-fat sour cream.

CHICKEN AND SHRIMP CARBONARA

Creamy dishes like pasta carbonara seem indulgent, but they don't have to be. Look to Toby's Tip for ways to make it a little healthier without compromising on flavor.

6 large pasteurized egg yolks, at room temperature

1 cup (250 mL) milk

Nonstick cooking spray

4 oz (125 g) bacon

1 large clove garlic, minced

8 oz (250 g) peeled and deveined large shrimp, tails removed

10 oz (300 g) dried spaghetti

1 cup (250 mL) shredded rotisserie chicken

¼ tsp (1 mL) freshly ground pepper

½ cup (125 mL) freshly grated Parmesan cheese

1. In a medium bowl, whisk together the egg yolks and milk. Set aside.

2. Coat a large sauté pan with nonstick cooking spray and heat over medium heat. When the oil is shimmering, add the bacon and cook until crisp and browned, 3 minutes on each side. Using a slotted spoon, remove the bacon and place on a paper towel to drain. When the bacon is cool enough to handle, dice.

3. Return the sauté pan with the bacon drippings to medium heat. Add the garlic and cook, stirring occasionally, until fragrant, 30 seconds. Add the shrimp and cook until the shrimp are pink, 3 minutes on each side. Remove from the pan and set aside.

4. Bring a 4-quart (4 L) stockpot of water to a boil over high heat. Add the spaghetti and boil gently until al dente, 8 minutes. Add ½ cup (125 mL) of pasta water to the egg mixture and stir until smooth. Drain the spaghetti and then immediately add back to the pasta pot. Pour the egg mixture over the pasta and stir to coat. Place the pot over low heat and gently stir the pasta until the sauce has thickened. Add the bacon, shrimp, chicken and pepper and toss to combine. Transfer the pasta to a large serving bowl and sprinkle with the cheese. Serve warm.

MAKE AHEAD: The bacon can be made the day before for this recipe, or use leftovers from breakfast.

SERVING SIZE: 1¾ cups (425 mL)

TOBY'S TIP: Lighten up this dish by using 2% milk and turkey bacon, and give it a nutritional boost by using whole wheat spaghetti.

MAC AND CHEESE
WITH CHICKEN

Adding rotisserie chicken to classic mac and cheese makes the dish more balanced by adding more protein. If you're feeling adventurous and want to add some veggies to your mac and cheese, add 1 to 2 cups (250 to 500 mL) chopped cooked cauliflower or finely diced roasted butternut squash.

PREHEAT THE OVEN TO 350°F (180°C)

Nonstick cooking spray

8 oz (250 g) elbow macaroni

6 tbsp (90 mL) unsalted butter, divided

¼ cup (60 mL) unbleached all-purpose flour

½ tsp (2 mL) dry mustard

½ tsp (2 mL) garlic powder

¼ tsp (1 mL) salt

⅛ tsp (0.5 mL) cayenne pepper

2 cups (500 mL) milk, at room temperature

1½ cups (375 mL) shredded sharp (old) Cheddar cheese, divided

1 cup (250 mL) chopped rotisserie chicken

1 cup (250 mL) panko bread crumbs

1. Coat an 8-inch (20 cm) square glass baking dish with nonstick cooking spray.

2. Bring a 3-quart (3 L) saucepan of water to a boil over high heat. Add the elbow macaroni, stir to combine, and boil gently until the pasta is al dente, 7 minutes. Drain and rinse in cool water. Set aside.

3. In a large saucepan over medium heat, melt 4 tbsp (60 mL) of the butter. Using a whisk, slowly add the flour and stir to prevent lumps. Add the mustard, garlic powder, salt and cayenne and cook for 1 minute, whisking occasionally. Add one-third of the milk while whisking. Continue adding one-third more milk while whisking, and then the remaining milk and whisk until smooth. Continue cooking for an additional 2 to 3 minutes. Add 1¼ cups (300 mL) of the Cheddar cheese and stir until combined and the mixture is smooth. Remove the saucepan from the heat. Gently fold in the macaroni and chicken until combined.

4. Gently pour the macaroni and cheese mixture into the prepared baking dish.

5. To make the bread crumbs, melt the remaining butter in a small saucepan over low heat. Add the panko bread crumbs and toss to coat, toasting the bread crumbs until lightly browned, about 2 minutes. Remove the pan from the heat. Sprinkle the remaining Cheddar cheese over the macaroni dish, and then sprinkle evenly with the bread crumbs.

6. Bake in the preheated oven until bubbling and golden brown, about 15 minutes. Remove from the oven and let cool for at least 10 minutes before serving.

SERVING SIZE: 2 cups (500 mL)

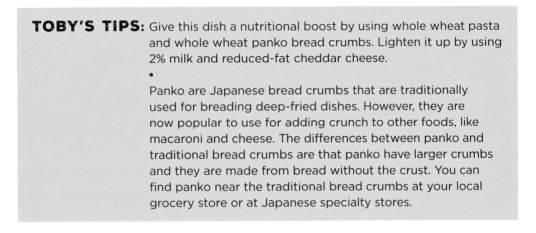

TOBY'S TIPS: Give this dish a nutritional boost by using whole wheat pasta and whole wheat panko bread crumbs. Lighten it up by using 2% milk and reduced-fat cheddar cheese.

•

Panko are Japanese bread crumbs that are traditionally used for breading deep-fried dishes. However, they are now popular to use for adding crunch to other foods, like macaroni and cheese. The differences between panko and traditional bread crumbs are that panko have larger crumbs and they are made from bread without the crust. You can find panko near the traditional bread crumbs at your local grocery store or at Japanese specialty stores.

CHICKEN AND CHEESE LASAGNA

This lasagna is a fantastic candidate for meal prepping. Make a batch on Sunday, slice it into eight pieces and freeze them individually. That way you can bring it to work for lunch and be the envy of your coworkers. The rotisserie chicken and no-boil noodles make assembling this lasagna a snap.

PREHEAT THE OVEN TO 350°F (180°C)

Nonstick cooking spray

¾ cup (175 mL) freshly grated Parmesan cheese, divided

1¼ cups (300 mL) ricotta cheese

2¾ cups (675 mL) shredded mozzarella cheese, divided

1 large egg, beaten

1 tbsp (15 mL) dried parsley

1 tbsp (15 mL) olive oil or canola oil

1 medium onion, chopped

2 cloves garlic, minced

4 cups (1 L) chopped rotisserie chicken

14-oz (398 mL) can diced tomatoes, with juice

2 tbsp (30 mL) tomato paste

1 tbsp (15 mL) dried oregano

2 tsp (10 mL) dried basil

¼ tsp (1 mL) salt

¼ tsp (1 mL) freshly ground black pepper

14-oz (398 mL) can tomato sauce, divided

9 oven-ready lasagna noodles

1. Coat an 11- by 14-inch (28 by 35 cm) baking dish with nonstick cooking spray.

2. In a medium bowl, stir together ½ cup (125 mL) of the Parmesan cheese, ricotta, ¾ cup (175 mL) of the mozzarella, egg and parsley.

3. Heat the oil in a large saucepan over medium heat. When the oil is shimmering, add the onion and garlic and cook, stirring occasionally, until the onion is translucent and the garlic is fragrant, 3 minutes. Add the chicken, diced tomatoes with juice, tomato paste, oregano, basil, salt and pepper and toss to combine. Raise the heat to medium-high and cook, stirring occasionally, until heated through, about 5 minutes.

4. Spoon ¼ cup (60 mL) of the tomato sauce on the bottom of the prepared baking dish, spreading it evenly with the back of a spoon.

5. Fill a large flat container with water. Dip each of 3 lasagna noodles in the water, shaking off the excess water. Place the noodles on the bottom of the baking dish side by side, overlapping them as little as possible. Top with half the cheese mixture followed by half the chicken mixture. Repeat the layers with the lasagna noodles dipped in water, followed by the remaining cheese mixture and remaining chicken mixture. Top with the last 3 noodles dipped in water, and spread the remaining tomato sauce over the noodles. Sprinkle the top with the remaining Parmesan cheese and the remaining mozzarella.

6. Cover the lasagna with foil and bake in the preheated oven for 35 to 40 minutes until the cheese has melted and the top is slightly browned. Uncover and bake for an additional 10 minutes. Remove the pan from the oven and let cool for at least 10 minutes before slicing into eight even pieces.

SERVING SIZE: 1 piece

TOBY'S TIPS: Lighten up this dish by using part-skim ricotta cheese and shredded part-skim mozzarella cheese, and give it a nutritional boost by using whole wheat pasta.

•

To cut back on sodium, look for no-salt-added diced tomatoes and tomato paste.

CHICKEN AND SPINACH STUFFED SHELLS

Cheesy stuffed shells are given a balancing boost with the added protein from rotisserie chicken plus vitamin-rich spinach. If you want to add even more vegetables, add one shredded carrot or ½ cup (125 mL) finely chopped broccoli to the cheese mixture.

PREHEAT THE OVEN TO 350°F (180°C)

Nonstick cooking spray

24 jumbo pasta shells

8 oz (250 g) frozen chopped spinach

8 oz (250 g) ricotta cheese

1 large egg, beaten

1 tsp (5 mL) dried parsley

½ tsp (2 mL) dried basil

¼ tsp (1 mL) salt

⅛ tsp (0.5 mL) hot pepper flakes

⅛ tsp (0.5 mL) freshly ground black pepper

2½ cups (625 mL) finely chopped rotisserie chicken

2 cups (500 mL) store-bought marinara sauce, divided

1 cup (250 mL) shredded mozzarella cheese

¼ cup (60 mL) freshly grated Parmesan cheese

1. Coat an 8- by 12-inch (20 by 30 cm) baking dish with nonstick cooking spray.

2. Bring a 4-quart (4 L) stockpot of water to a boil over high heat. Add the pasta shells, and gently boil, stirring occasionally, until al dente, about 7 minutes. Drain the pasta completely and set it aside (do not rinse).

3. Fill a medium saucepan with 1 cup (250 mL) water and bring to a boil over high heat. Add the spinach and lower the heat to medium-low. Cook, stirring occasionally, until tender, 5 minutes. Drain the spinach, and set it aside to slightly cool, about 5 minutes. Using clean hands or a clean cloth, squeeze out excess water.

4. In a large bowl, stir together the ricotta, egg, parsley, basil, salt, pepper flakes and black pepper. Add the spinach and chicken and stir to combine.

5. Spread 1 cup (250 mL) of the marinara sauce over the bottom of the prepared baking dish.

6. Spoon 2 tbsp (30 mL) of the cheese mixture into each pasta shell. Arrange the stuffed shells in a single layer with the seam side up, leaving space between them, in the prepared baking dish. Top with the remaining marinara sauce and sprinkle with the mozzarella cheese and the Parmesan cheese. Bake in the preheated oven until lightly browned and cooked through, 20 minutes. Remove from the oven and let cool for 10 minutes before serving.

MAKE AHEAD: Shells can be cooked 1 to 2 days in advance and stored in the fridge until use.

SERVING SIZE: 4 stuffed shells

TOBY'S TIPS: Lighten up this dish by using part-skim ricotta cheese and shredded part-skim mozzarella cheese.

•

Serve with Honey Roasted Carrots (page 158), Sheet Pan Vegetables (page 160) or a green tossed salad on the side.

CHICKEN AND MUSHROOM BAKED RISOTTO

This method for making risotto is a little unconventional, but it tastes just as amazing as traditional risotto. Instead of the typical need to sit over your pan stirring for 40 minutes, the oven does all the work. Use this extra time to catch up with your family or to kick back and relax before dinner.

PREHEAT THE OVEN TO 350°F (180°C)

2 tbsp (30 mL) unsalted butter

2 tbsp (30 mL) olive oil

1 lb (500 g) cremini mushrooms, thinly sliced

⅓ cup (75 mL) diced shallots

2 cloves garlic, minced

1 tsp (5 mL) dried thyme

1½ cups (375 mL) Arborio rice

2 cups (500 mL) reduced-sodium ready-to-use chicken broth, warmed

½ cup (125 mL) white cooking wine or dry white wine

¼ tsp (1 mL) salt

¼ cup (60 mL) freshly grated Parmesan cheese

2 cups (500 mL) shredded rotisserie chicken

1. In a large sauté pan over medium heat, melt the butter and oil. Add the mushrooms and cook, stirring occasionally, until browned, 6 minutes. Add the shallots, garlic and thyme and cook, stirring occasionally, until the shallots soften and the garlic is fragrant, 2 minutes. Add the rice and toss with the mushroom mixture until combined. Add the chicken broth, cooking wine and salt, raise the heat and bring to a boil. Cover the sauté pan and carefully place in the preheated oven. Bake the risotto, without mixing, for 30 minutes. Using an oven mitt, carefully remove the pan from the oven and place on the stove. Stir the rice over medium heat until creamy, about 5 minutes. Add the Parmesan cheese and chicken and toss to combine. Serve warm.

SERVING SIZE: 2½ cups (625 mL)

> **TOBY'S TIP:** You can find cremini mushrooms sold as "baby bella" or "baby portobello" mushrooms. They are all the same mushroom.

SWEET POTATO CHICKEN CHILI

Chili is one of the best dishes to customize with whatever vegetables you happen to have on hand. For example, I love adding potatoes of all types, such as russet potatoes or sweet potatoes, which hold up well in this dish. You can also add peas, edamame, parsnips, turnips or other beans — anything goes!

2 tbsp (30 mL) olive oil or canola oil

1 small yellow onion, diced

1½ lbs (750 g) sweet potatoes, peeled and cut into ½-inch (1 cm) cubes (4 cups/1 L)

1 tbsp (15 mL) chili powder

2 tsp (10 mL) ground cumin

1 tsp (5 mL) smoked paprika

½ tsp (2 mL) salt

¼ tsp (1 mL) freshly ground black pepper

⅛ tsp (0.5 mL) ground cinnamon

28-oz (796 mL) can crushed tomatoes, with juice

1 cup (250 mL) reduced-sodium ready-to-use chicken broth

15 oz (425 g) frozen corn kernels, thawed

14- to 19-oz (398 to 540 mL) can reduced-sodium black beans, drained and rinsed

2 cups (500 mL) coarsely chopped rotisserie chicken

1. Heat the oil in a large pot over medium heat. When the oil is shimmering, add the onion and sauté until soft and translucent, 3 minutes. Add the sweet potatoes, chili powder, cumin, paprika, salt, pepper and cinnamon and toss to combine. Cook, stirring occasionally, until the mixture is fragrant, 1 to 2 minutes. Stir in the crushed tomatoes with juice, chicken broth, corn and beans. Raise the heat to high and bring the mixture to a boil. Lower the heat to medium-low, cover and simmer, stirring occasionally, until the potatoes are tender and the mixture has thickened, about 25 minutes. Add the chicken, increase the heat to high and bring to a boil. Then lower the heat to medium and cook, uncovered, stirring occasionally, until the chicken is heated through, about 3 minutes.

SERVING SIZE: About 2 cups (500 mL)

TOBY'S TIP: When selecting sweet potatoes, choose those that are firm with intact skin without blemishes or large dents. Store in a cool, dry place for up to 1 month.

EASY CHICKEN AND SAUSAGE PAELLA

This Spanish-inspired rice dish is made with a colorful spice called saffron. This spice has a deep orange hue and subtle flavor that makes this dish oh-so-delicious. The addition of chorizo and rotisserie chicken, along with vegetables, make it a one-pot meal that everyone will love.

3 cups (750 mL) reduced-sodium ready-to-use chicken broth

⅛ tsp (0.5 mL) saffron (see Toby's Tips)

Nonstick cooking spray

8 oz (250 g) chorizo, sliced into rounds and then quartered

1 tbsp (15 mL) olive oil

1 yellow onion, chopped

3 cloves garlic, minced

1 green bell pepper, diced

2 tsp (10 mL) sweet paprika

1½ cups (375 mL) short-grain white rice

1½ cups (375 mL) chopped plum (Roma) tomatoes

2 cups (500 mL) shredded rotisserie chicken

1 cup (250 mL) frozen green peas

2 lemons, cut into thick wedges to serve

1. In a medium saucepan, bring the broth to a boil over high heat. Stir in the saffron and set aside to steep.

2. Coat a large sauté pan with nonstick cooking spray and set over medium heat. When the oil is shimmering, add the chorizo and cook, turning halfway through, until brown and crispy, about 4 minutes. Using a slotted spoon, remove the chorizo and allow to cool. Once the chorizo is cool enough to handle, chop and place into a small bowl.

3. In the same pan with the chorizo drippings, heat the olive oil over medium heat. When the oil is shimmering, add the onion and garlic and cook, stirring occasionally, until the onion is translucent and the garlic is fragrant, 3 minutes. Add the green pepper and sweet paprika, stir to combine and cook for 1 more minute. Add the rice and toss to combine. Add the tomatoes and broth mixture and stir to combine. Raise the heat to high and bring to a boil, then reduce the heat and bring down to a simmer. Cover the pan and cook on low for 15 to 20 minutes without stirring. Remove the lid and add the chicken, peas and chorizo and gently fold into the rice. Cover the pan and cook for another 5 minutes, or until all the liquid is absorbed and the rice is tender. If all the broth evaporates and the rice is still underdone, add ½ cup (125 mL) water and cover and check in 5 minutes. Serve warm with lemon wedges.

SERVING SIZE: 1⅓ cups (325 mL)

TOBY'S TIPS: Give the paella a nutritional boost by using short-grain brown rice in place of the white rice. Increase the cooking time to 40 minutes in step 3, once the pan is simmering.

•

Lighten up this dish by reducing the amount of chorizo in the recipe. You can also easily swap the chorizo for chicken, turkey or plant-based sausage or use an additional 1¼ cups (300 mL) of rotisserie chicken instead.

•

Saffron is a little different than most spices in your spice drawer. This dark orange, threadlike spice is harvested by drying the stigma of the *Crocus sativus* flower over heat. It takes more than two hundred thousand crocus stigmas to make 1 pound (500 g) of saffron, which is why it is so pricey. Less expensive saffron is mixed with other substances that are similar in color, like marigold. You only need a small amount in recipes (like ⅛ tsp/0.5 mL in this recipe), so invest in good-quality saffron as it will last a while.

MAKES 4 SERVINGS

SOUTHWEST CHICKEN AND RICE STUFFED PEPPERS

My grandmother used to make stuffed peppers in a traditional style from her Romanian childhood with white rice and ground beef (and sometimes even dried apricots and raisins). This version combines the Southwest flavors I love — beans, corn, rice and chili powder — with the dish I grew up loving.

1 cup (250 mL) reduced-sodium ready-to-use chicken broth

½ cup (125 mL) long-grain white rice

Nonstick cooking spray

4 green bell peppers

1 tbsp (15 mL) olive oil

1 yellow onion, diced

2 cloves garlic, minced

1 cup (250 mL) tomato purée

1 cup (250 mL) frozen corn, thawed, or fresh corn

1 cup (250 mL) canned reduced-sodium black beans, rinsed and drained

1 tbsp (15 mL) chili powder

2 tsp (10 mL) ground cumin

¼ tsp (1 mL) salt

⅛ tsp (0.5 mL) hot pepper flakes

2 cups (500 mL) chopped rotisserie chicken

1 cup (250 mL) shredded Cheddar cheese

1. To make the rice, add the chicken broth and rice to a medium saucepan and bring to a boil over high heat. Lower the heat to medium-low and simmer, covered, until the rice is cooked, 15 to 20 minutes. Set aside to slightly cool.

2. Preheat oven to 350°F (180°C). Coat an 11- by 8-inch (28 by 20 cm) glass baking dish with nonstick cooking spray.

3. Slice the green peppers in half from the top down and hollow out the seeds and ribs. Place in the prepared baking dish cut side up.

4. Heat the oil in a large sauté pan over medium heat. When the oil is shimmering, add the onion and garlic and cook, stirring occasionally, until the onion is soft and translucent and the garlic is fragrant, 3 minutes. Add the cooked rice, tomato purée, corn, beans, chili powder, cumin, salt and pepper flakes and stir to combine. Cook until warmed through, about 3 minutes. Add the chicken and gently mix to incorporate.

5. Divide the mixture evenly into each of the pepper halves. Bake in the oven for 15 minutes and then carefully remove the baking dish and sprinkle the cheese evenly over the pepper halves. Return the baking dish to the oven and continue baking until the pepper is soft and the cheese has melted, 15 minutes. Remove the peppers from the oven and set aside to slightly cool before serving.

SERVING SIZE: 2 pepper halves

TOBY'S TIPS: Give these peppers a nutritional boost by using long-grain brown rice in place of the white rice. Increase the cooking time to 40 minutes in step 1, once the pan is simmering.

Lighten up this dish by using shredded reduced-fat Cheddar cheese.

For something different, swap the bell peppers for heirloom tomatoes and cook until the tomatoes have slightly softened, about 10 minutes. Use a spoon to scoop out the insides of the tomatoes to hollow.

NORTH AFRICAN CHICKEN AND QUINOA

Large chunks of vegetables, chicken, spices and quinoa make up this delicious dish. Take advantage of the cook time on this quick-to-prep recipe by whipping up an easy green tossed salad and setting the table for dinner.

PREHEAT THE OVEN TO 400°F (200°C)
OVENPROOF SKILLET

2 tbsp (30 mL) olive oil

2 cloves garlic, minced

1½ tsp (7 mL) ground cumin

1½ tsp (7 mL) sweet paprika

½ tsp (2 mL) ground coriander

½ tsp (2 mL) ground turmeric

¼ tsp (1 mL) salt

⅛ tsp (0.5 mL) ground cinnamon

1 lb (500 g) Yukon gold potatoes, cut into 1½-inch (4 cm) cubes

6 medium carrots, peeled and cut into 2-inch (5 cm) pieces

1 large red onion, cut into 8 wedges

1 jalapeño pepper, seeded and cut into ¼-inch (0.5 cm) slices

3 cups (750 mL) reduced-sodium ready-to-use chicken broth

¼ cup (60 mL) harissa

2 tbsp (30 mL) tomato paste

2 cups (500 mL) quinoa

2 cups (500 mL) shredded rotisserie chicken

1. In a small bowl, whisk together the oil, garlic, cumin, paprika, coriander, turmeric, salt and cinnamon.

2. In a large bowl, add the potatoes, carrots, red onion and jalapeño. Drizzle the oil mixture over the vegetables and toss to coat. Place the vegetables in a single layer in an ovenproof skillet and bake in the preheated oven until the edges have browned, 20 to 25 minutes. Using oven mitts, transfer the skillet from the oven to the stove.

3. In a medium bowl, whisk together the chicken broth, harissa and tomato paste.

4. Add the quinoa to the pan of vegetables and toss gently. Add the broth mixture and gently stir until well combined. Turn on the heat to high and bring the skillet to a boil, then reduce the heat to medium-low and simmer, covered, until the quinoa is cooked through and the vegetables have softened, 10 minutes. Fold in the chicken and cook until the quinoa is tender and the chicken is heated through, 5 minutes.

SERVING SIZE: 2 cups (500 mL)

CHICKEN FAJITA BOWLS

Instead of heading to a quick-service Mexican joint for a bowl, you can easily make your own at home. This dish contains rice, chicken and sautéed vegetables. Add some black beans if that's a must-have in your fajita bowl!

3 tbsp (45 mL) olive oil or canola oil

1 clove garlic, minced

1 tsp (5 mL) smoked paprika

½ tsp (2 mL) ground cumin

½ tsp (2 mL) salt, divided

¼ tsp (1 mL) freshly ground black pepper, divided

2 cups (500 mL) reduced-sodium ready-to-use chicken broth

1 cup (250 mL) long-grain white rice

Nonstick cooking spray

1 yellow bell pepper, seeded and sliced into ¼-inch (0.5 cm) strips

1 red bell pepper, seeded and sliced into ¼-inch (0.5 cm) strips

1 onion, thinly sliced

4 cups (1 L) shredded rotisserie chicken

2 tbsp (30 mL) chopped fresh cilantro

1. In a medium bowl, whisk together the oil, garlic, smoked paprika, cumin, ¼ tsp (1 mL) of the salt and ⅛ tsp (0.5 mL) of the black pepper.

2. Add the chicken broth and rice to a medium saucepan and bring to a boil over high heat. Lower the heat to medium-low and simmer, covered, until the rice is cooked, 15 to 20 minutes. Set aside to cool.

3. Coat a medium sauté pan with nonstick cooking spray and heat over medium heat. When the oil is shimmering, add the yellow and red peppers and onion and cook, stirring occasionally, until softened, 5 minutes. Toss with the remaining salt and black pepper. Transfer the vegetables to a clean bowl and set aside.

4. In the same sauté pan over medium heat, add the chicken and smoked paprika mixture and toss to combine. Cook, stirring occasionally, until the chicken is heated through, 5 minutes.

5. To assemble the bowls, scoop ½ cup (125 mL) of the rice into each of four bowls. Next to the rice add 1 cup (250 mL) of the chicken mixture and one-quarter of the vegetables. Sprinkle each bowl with 1½ tsp (7 mL) of the cilantro.

MAKE AHEAD: The rice can be made up to 5 days in advance and stored in the refrigerator in a sealable container. Warm the rice in the microwave on High for 30 seconds before assembling the bowls.

SERVING SIZE: 1 bowl

GREEK CHICKEN AND RICE BOWLS

Bowls, like this one, are popular for a good reason. These dishes combine a few simple components in a bowl to create a delicious masterpiece. In this Greek-inspired bowl you have rice, an easy chopped salad, rotisserie chicken seasoned with Greek spices and tzatziki (a yogurt-based sauce). Once you get the hang of it, you can start experimenting with making your own creations.

RICE

2 cups (500 mL) reduced-sodium ready-to-use chicken broth

1 cup (250 mL) long-grain white rice

SALAD

1 English (hothouse) cucumber, chopped

2 plum (Roma) tomatoes, chopped

¼ cup (60 mL) pitted kalamata olives, halved lengthwise

¼ cup (60 mL) crumbled feta cheese

1 tbsp (15 mL) extra virgin olive oil

Juice of 1 lemon

¼ tsp salt (1 mL)

⅛ tsp (0.5 mL) freshly ground black pepper

CHICKEN

1 tbsp (15 mL) olive oil or canola oil

1 clove garlic, minced

4 cups (1 L) shredded rotisserie chicken

Juice of 1 lemon

1 tsp (5 mL) dried rosemary

1 tsp (5 mL) dried thyme

1 tsp (5 mL) dried oregano

¼ tsp (1 mL) salt

⅛ tsp (0.5 mL) freshly ground black pepper

½ cup (125 mL) Tzatziki Sauce (page 179) or store-bought tzatziki

1. **RICE:** Add the chicken broth and rice to a medium saucepan and bring to a boil over high heat. Lower the heat to medium-low and simmer, covered, until the rice is cooked, 15 to 20 minutes. Set aside to slightly cool.

2. **SALAD:** In a medium bowl, toss together the cucumbers, tomatoes and olives. Add the feta cheese, oil, lemon juice, salt and pepper and toss to combine.

3. **CHICKEN:** Heat the oil in a medium saucepan over medium heat. When the oil is shimmering, add the garlic and cook, stirring occasionally, until fragrant, 30 seconds. Add the chicken, lemon juice, rosemary, thyme, oregano, salt and pepper and toss to combine. Cook until the chicken is heated through, 5 minutes.

4. To assemble the bowl, scoop ½ cup (125 mL) of the rice into each of four bowls. Next, spoon 1 cup (250 mL) of the chicken mixture next to the rice in each bowl and place about 1 cup (250 mL) of the salad alongside it. Top the salad with 2 tbsp (30 mL) of the Tzatziki Sauce.

MAKE AHEAD: Make the rice ahead of time and store in the refrigerator for up to 5 days before use. Reheat on the stovetop or microwave before adding to the bowl.

SERVING SIZE: 1 bowl

TOBY'S TIPS: Give this healthy dish an even bigger nutritional boost by using long-grain brown rice in place of the white rice. Increase the cooking time to 40 minutes in step 1, once the pan is simmering.

The chopped salad pairs nicely with many dishes, including Sweet Potato Chicken Chili (page 109) and Chicken Loaf (page 119). You can also omit the feta cheese and olives from the salad and just use the chopped vegetables.

GARLIC SMOTHERED CHICKEN

There's nothing better than the smell of roasted garlic filling up your kitchen. This mouthwatering dish smothers rotisserie chicken with an entire bulb of roasted garlic and fresh tomatoes and finishes it off with the bright flavor of white wine.

PREHEAT THE OVEN TO 400°F (200°C)

1 bulb garlic

2 tbsp (30 mL) olive oil, divided

4 cups (1 L) shredded rotisserie chicken

2 cups (500 mL) chopped plum (Roma) tomatoes

½ cup (125 mL) white cooking wine or dry white wine

½ tsp (2 mL) dried thyme

½ tsp (2 mL) dried oregano

¼ tsp (1 mL) salt

⅛ tsp (0.5 mL) freshly ground black pepper

1. Using a sharp knife, cut the bulb of garlic about ½ inch (1 cm) from the top so some of the cloves are visible. Drizzle with 1 tbsp (15 mL) of the oil and wrap in foil. Place the bulb in the oven and roast until the garlic is lightly brown, 30 minutes. Set aside to cool for 10 minutes.

2. Remove the garlic cloves from the bulb and place in a medium bowl. Add the chicken and toss to coat the chicken.

3. Heat the remaining oil in a large sauté pan over medium heat. When the oil is shimmering, add the chicken and tomatoes and toss to combine. Add the wine, thyme, oregano, salt and pepper and bring the mixture to a boil. Reduce the heat to medium-low and simmer, stirring occasionally, until the flavors combine and the chicken is heated through, 5 minutes.

SERVING SIZE: 1¼ cups (300 mL)

TOBY'S TIP: When selecting fresh garlic, choose bulbs that are firm and tight. Store them in an open or ventilated container in a cool, dry place for up to 3 months. Once you begin using the cloves in the bulb, use within 2 weeks.

CHICKEN LOAF

Give classic meatloaf a simple twist with rotisserie chicken. Mince the rotisserie in a blender, mix it up with the other ingredients and bake. Violà! Dinner is done.

PREHEAT THE OVEN TO 400°F (200°C)
BLENDER, INSTANT-READ THERMOMETER

Nonstick cooking spray

¼ cup (60 mL) ketchup

1 tbsp (15 mL) Dijon mustard

2 tsp (10 mL) brown sugar

3 cups (750 mL) shredded rotisserie chicken

14- to 19-oz (398 to 540 mL) can reduced-sodium cannellini beans, drained and rinsed

¾ cup (175 mL) large-flake (old-fashioned) rolled oats

1 yellow onion, chopped

2 carrots, shredded

2 cloves garlic, minced

1 large egg, beaten

14-oz (398 mL) can petite diced tomatoes, with juice

1 tbsp (15 mL) Worcestershire sauce

1 tsp (5 mL) dried parsley

¼ tsp (1 mL) salt

¼ tsp (1 mL) dried sage

⅛ tsp (0.5 mL) freshly ground black pepper

1. Coat a 9- by 5-inch (23 by 12.5 cm) loaf pan with nonstick cooking spray.

2. In a small bowl, whisk together the ketchup, Dijon mustard and brown sugar.

3. Place the chicken and beans in a blender and pulse several times until the mixture is finely minced. Spoon the mixture into a large bowl. Add the oats, onion, carrots, garlic, egg, tomatoes with juice, Worcestershire sauce, parsley, salt, sage and pepper. Using clean hands, mix well until the ingredients are combined.

4. Place the chicken mixture into the prepared loaf pan, making sure the top is level. Pour the ketchup mixture over the loaf, using a spatula or the back of a wooden spoon to spread it evenly.

5. Bake the loaf until an instant-read thermometer inserted into the center reads 165°F (75°C), 45 to 50 minutes. Remove from the oven and let cool for 10 minutes before cutting into eight even slices. Serve warm.

SERVING SIZE: 1 slice

TOBY'S TIP: Serve with Garlic Sautéed Spinach (page 163) and Israeli Couscous and Mushrooms (page 164).

CHICKEN POT PIE

Using rotisserie chicken is a great time-saver when preparing this popular comfort food. Because you're using precooked chicken, you'll save at least 20 minutes of prep and cook time. This just means you can whip up this dinnertime classic more often!

PREHEAT THE OVEN TO 400°F (200°C)

FILLING

Nonstick cooking spray

2 tbsp (30 mL) canola oil

1 yellow onion, chopped

1 clove garlic, minced

4 oz (125 g) cremini mushrooms, thinly sliced

¼ cup (60 mL) unbleached all-purpose flour

1½ cups (375 mL) reduced-sodium ready-to-use chicken broth

1½ cups (375 mL) milk

1½ cups (375 mL) chopped rotisserie chicken

1½ cups (375 mL) frozen peas and carrots, thawed

¾ cup (175 mL) frozen green beans, thawed

2 tsp (10 mL) dried parsley

½ tsp (2 mL) dried thyme

¼ tsp (1 mL) salt

⅛ tsp (0.5 mL) freshly ground black pepper

TOPPING

1 tbsp (15 mL) freshly grated Parmesan cheese

¼ tsp (1 mL) dried thyme

1½ cups (375 mL) unbleached all-purpose flour

1¼ tsp (6 mL) baking powder

¾ tsp (3 mL) baking soda

½ tsp (2 mL) salt

4 tbsp (60 mL) cold butter, cut into small pieces

1 cup (250 mL) low-fat buttermilk

1. Coat an 8-inch (20 cm) pie plate with nonstick cooking spray.

2. FILLING: Heat the oil in a large skillet over medium heat. When the oil is shimmering, add the onion and garlic and cook, stirring occasionally, until the onion is translucent and the garlic is fragrant, 3 minutes. Add the mushrooms and sauté until they soften, about 5 minutes. Sprinkle the mixture with the flour and cook, stirring occasionally, for 1 minute. Slowly add the broth and milk and whisk until combined. Add the chicken, peas and carrots and green beans, raise the heat to medium-high and bring back to a gentle boil. Reduce the heat to medium-low and simmer, stirring occasionally, until the mixture is thick and creamy, about 8 minutes. Stir in the parsley, thyme, salt and pepper.

3. Place the prepared pie plate onto a baking sheet. Carefully pour the mixture into the prepared pie plate and set aside.

4. TOPPING: In a small bowl, mix together the Parmesan cheese and thyme.

5. In a medium bowl, sift together the all-purpose flour, baking powder, baking soda and salt. Using clean fingers, mix the butter into the flour mixture until the butter is incorporated and crumbly and no pieces are larger than a pea. Gently stir in the buttermilk until combined — do not overmix.

6. Drop the biscuit dough onto the filled pie plate in six even $\frac{1}{2}$-cup (125 mL) scoops. Sprinkle with the Parmesan cheese mixture. Bake in the preheated oven until the top is slightly browned, about 30 minutes. Remove the pot pie from the oven and let cool for 10 minutes before slicing into six even pieces.

SERVING SIZE: $\frac{1}{6}$ pie

TOBY'S TIPS: Lighten up this recipe by using 2% milk.

The biscuit topping uses all-purpose flour. To add more fiber, use $\frac{3}{4}$ cup (175 mL) each all-purpose flour and whole wheat pastry flour (or white whole wheat flour).

SPAGHETTI SQUASH CHICKEN PARM BAKE

Once you open and cook the squash, you'll be amazed how similar to spaghetti the strands truly are. You can also use the empty spaghetti squash shells to serve the dish — it'll help save some dishes.

PREHEAT THE OVEN TO 375°F (190°C)

Nonstick cooking spray

1 spaghetti squash, approximately 3 lbs (1.5 kg)

1 tbsp (15 mL) olive oil

2 cups (500 mL) chopped rotisserie chicken

14-oz (398 mL) can diced tomatoes, with juice

1½ cups (375 mL) store-bought marinara sauce, divided

½ cup (125 mL) freshly grated Parmesan cheese, divided

1 tsp (5 mL) garlic powder

1 tsp (5 mL) dried parsley

½ tsp (2 mL) dried basil

¼ tsp (1 mL) salt

⅛ tsp (0.5 mL) freshly ground black pepper

⅛ tsp (0.5 mL) hot pepper flakes

1 cup (250 mL) shredded mozzarella cheese

1. Coat a baking sheet with nonstick cooking spray. Coat a 9- by 11-inch (23 by 28 cm) glass baking dish with cooking spray.

2. Using a fork, poke several holes in the spaghetti squash. Microwave on High for 5 minutes. Let cool for 2 minutes, then, using a sharp knife, slice the spaghetti squash lengthwise. If the squash is still too tough to slice, microwave for an additional 5 minutes.

3. Place the squash halves, cut sides down, onto the prepared baking sheet. Bake until the squash is easily pierced with a fork, 40 minutes. Remove from the oven and let cool for 10 minutes. Once cool enough to handle, use a spoon to scoop out the seeds. Use a fork to scrape the flesh to create spaghetti-like strands.

4. In a large mixing bowl, toss together the spaghetti squash and oil. Add the chicken, diced tomatoes with juice, 1 cup (250 mL) of the marinara sauce, ¼ cup (60 mL) of the Parmesan cheese, garlic powder, parsley, basil, salt, pepper and pepper flakes. Toss to combine. Pour the mixture into the prepared glass baking dish, making sure the top is level. Pour the remaining marinara sauce over the top and sprinkle with the mozzarella cheese and remaining Parmesan cheese. Bake in the preheated oven until the cheese has melted and browned, about 20 minutes.

SERVING SIZE: 2 cups (500 mL)

TOBY'S TIPS: Lighten up this dish by using shredded part-skim mozzarella cheese.

•

Spaghetti squash makes a great substitute for pasta. Swap it for the spaghetti in the Chicken and Shrimp Carbonara (page 101).

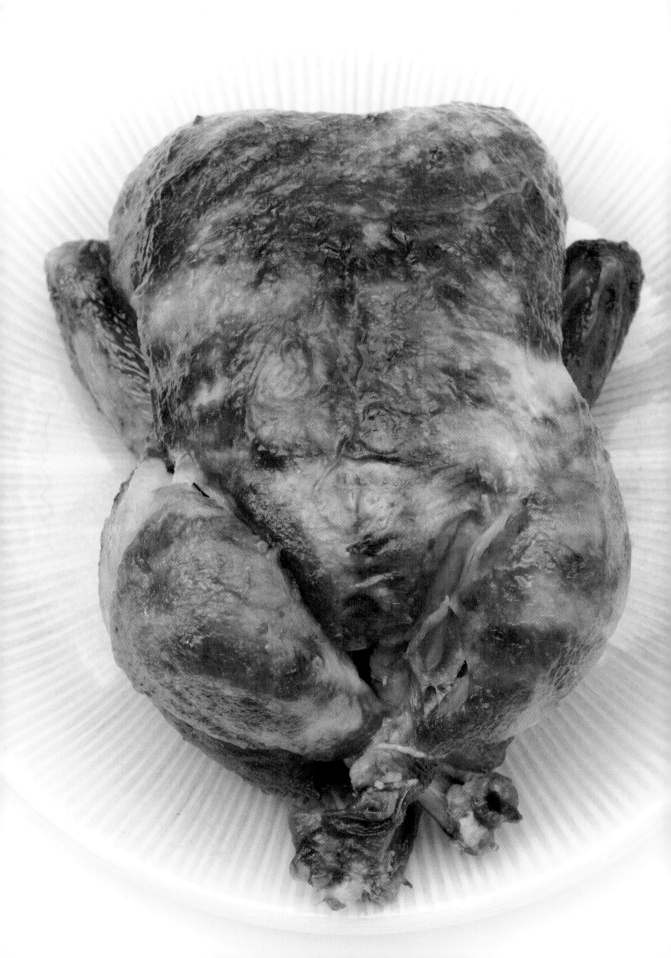

CHAPTER 8

EVEN EASIER MAINS

PESTO PASTA WITH CHICKEN

Whip up a homemade pesto, smother your pasta and add some vegetables and rotisserie chicken — it's a simple, tasty dinner. Use the vegetables called for in this recipe or substitute whatever you have on hand to help reduce food waste in your kitchen. Bell peppers, broccoli, cauliflower, kale or zucchini work well in this dish.

8 oz (250 g) fusilli pasta

1 tbsp (15 mL) olive oil

1 clove garlic, minced

2 cups (500 mL) fresh spinach

2 cups (500 mL) grape tomatoes, halved

2 cups (500 mL) shredded rotisserie chicken

¾ cup (175 mL) Easy Pesto Sauce (page 177) or store-bought pesto sauce

¼ cup (60 mL) freshly grated Parmesan cheese

1. Bring a 3-quart (3 L) stockpot of water to a boil over high heat. Add the pasta and cook until the pasta is fork-tender, 9 to 11 minutes. Drain and set aside to slightly cool.

2. In a large skillet, heat the oil over medium heat until shimmering. Add the garlic, spinach and tomatoes; cook, stirring occasionally, until the spinach has wilted and the tomatoes are softened, about 4 minutes. Add the chicken and toss to heat through. Reduce the heat to low, and then add the pasta and pesto, tossing to combine. Serve sprinkled with the Parmesan cheese.

SERVING SIZE: 1½ cups (375 mL)

TOBY'S TIPS: Give this dish a nutritional boost by using whole wheat fusilli pasta.

•

Or you can switch it up by using the same pesto sauce with spaghetti squash in place of the pasta. Just use the same method to cook and prep the spaghetti squash in the Spaghetti Squash Chicken Parm Bake (page 122).

MEDITERRANEAN ORZO AND CHICKEN

This dish is filled with delicious Mediterranean flavors like tomatoes, olives and feta cheese. Combined with fresh vegetables and rotisserie chicken, this mouthwatering meal will make regular appearances in your easy weeknight dinner repertoire.

10 oz (300g) orzo pasta

1 tbsp (15 mL) olive oil or canola oil

1 onion, chopped

1 clove garlic, minced

1 green bell pepper, sliced into ¼-inch (0.5 cm) strips

1 yellow bell pepper, sliced into ¼-inch (0.5 cm) strips

10 oz (300 g) white mushrooms, thinly sliced

28-oz (796 mL) can crushed tomatoes, with juice

4 cups (1 L) shredded rotisserie chicken

3 cups (750 mL) baby spinach

⅓ cup (75 mL) pitted kalamata olives, halved

¼ tsp (1 mL) salt

⅛ tsp (0.5 mL) freshly ground black pepper

¼ cup (60 mL) crumbled feta cheese

1. Bring a large pot of water to a boil over high heat, add the orzo and cook for 9 minutes or until al dente. Drain and transfer the orzo to a large serving bowl.

2. In a large skillet, heat the oil over medium heat until shimmering. Add the onion and cook, stirring, for 3 minutes or until translucent. Add the garlic and cook, stirring, for 30 seconds or until fragrant. Add the green pepper, yellow pepper and mushrooms; cook, stirring, for 6 minutes or until the vegetables are starting to soften.

3. Stir in the tomatoes with juice, chicken, spinach and olives; bring to a boil. Reduce the heat to medium-low, cover and simmer for 7 minutes or until the spinach is wilted and the flavors are blended. Stir in the salt and pepper. Sprinkle with the feta. Serve over orzo.

SERVING SIZE: 1⅓ cups (325 mL) chicken mixture, plus 1 cup (250 mL) orzo

TOBY'S TIP: Swap the orzo for the same amount of riced cauliflower, whole wheat couscous or quinoa.

THAI-STYLE CHICKEN CURRY

This vibrant Thai-style curry incorporates coconut milk, curry paste, soy sauce, fish sauce, turmeric and ginger in a stew-like dish. Instead of ordering it at a restaurant, make it yourself in 15 minutes using your precooked rotisserie chicken.

1 tbsp (15 mL) olive oil or canola oil

1 yellow onion, chopped

1 clove garlic, minced

4 cups (1 L) shredded rotisserie chicken

½ cup (125 mL) light canned coconut milk

½ cup (125 mL) reduced-sodium ready-to-use chicken broth

1 tbsp (15 mL) Thai red curry paste

1 tbsp (15 mL) reduced-sodium soy sauce

1 tsp (5 mL) fish sauce (nam pla)

1 tsp (5 mL) ground turmeric

¼ tsp (1 mL) ground ginger

1. In a medium saucepan, heat the oil over medium heat. When the oil is shimmering, add the onion and garlic and cook until fragrant, 2 minutes. Add the chicken, coconut milk, chicken broth, curry paste, soy sauce, fish sauce, turmeric and ginger and raise the heat to high to bring to a boil. Reduce the heat to low, cover and simmer until the flavors combine, 8 minutes. Serve warm.

SERVING SIZE: 1 cup (250 mL)

TOBY'S TIP: Serve the Thai-Style Chicken Curry over Brown Rice with Peas and Carrots (page 165).

PEANUT CHICKEN AND QUINOA BOWLS
WITH BROCCOLI

Bowls are an easy way to have a filling, nutritious meal, any time of the day. Combine a grain, vegetable and protein and top with a sauce or dressing of your choice, and you've got a well-balanced bowl! It's a good way to use leftover rotisserie chicken or even last night's vegetables, which also helps reduce food waste in your home.

1 cup (250 mL) quinoa

2 cups (500 mL) reduced-sodium ready-to-use chicken or vegetable broth

2 green onions, chopped

1 cup (250 mL) cherry tomatoes, halved

¼ tsp (1 mL) salt

2 cups (500 mL) broccoli florets

2 cups (500 mL) shredded rotisserie chicken, warmed

½ cup (125 mL) Spicy Peanut Sauce (page 180) or store-bought peanut sauce

¼ cup (60 mL) chopped fresh cilantro, divided

1. In a medium saucepan, bring the quinoa and chicken broth to a boil over high heat. Reduce the heat to low, cover the pan and simmer until all the liquid has been absorbed, 12 to 15 minutes. Remove the pan from the heat and fluff the quinoa with a fork. Add the green onions, tomatoes and salt and toss to combine.

2. Pour 1 cup (250 mL) of water into a medium pot fitted with a steamer basket, and bring the water to a boil over high heat. Add the broccoli, cover and steam until tender, 4 to 5 minutes. Remove the pot from the heat, remove the steamer basket and set the broccoli aside.

3. In each of four bowls, spoon ¾ cup (175 mL) quinoa, top with ½ cup (125 mL) chicken and place ½ cup (125 mL) broccoli on the side. Drizzle 2 tbsp (30 mL) of the peanut sauce over the contents of the bowl and sprinkle with 1 tbsp (15 mL) of the cilantro. Serve warm or cold.

SERVING SIZE: 1 bowl

TOBY'S TIP: Swap the broccoli for string beans or cauliflower.

WHITE BEAN AND CHICKEN CHILI

Speed up your dinnertime prep for this chili with two ready-made ingredients: rotisserie chicken and canned white beans. This will get a hearty bowl of chili on your table in 30 minutes or less.

1 tbsp (15 mL) olive oil or canola oil

1 onion, diced

2 cloves garlic, minced

Four 4½-oz (127 mL) cans chopped green chiles, drained

Two 14- to 19-oz (398 to 540 mL) cans reduced-sodium cannellini beans, drained and rinsed

1 tbsp (15 mL) ground cumin

2 tsp (10 mL) ground coriander

1 tsp (5 mL) chili powder

¼ tsp (1 mL) salt

⅛ tsp (0.5 mL) freshly ground black pepper

3 cups (750 mL) reduced-sodium ready-to-use chicken broth

4 cups (1 L) shredded rotisserie chicken

TOPPINGS (OPTIONAL)

Sour cream or plain Greek yogurt

Chopped fresh cilantro

1. Heat the oil in a large skillet over medium heat. When the oil is shimmering, add the onion and garlic and cook, stirring occasionally, until translucent, 3 minutes. Add the green chiles, beans, cumin, coriander, chili powder, salt and pepper and toss to combine. Add the chicken broth and bring the mixture to a boil. Lower the heat and simmer, stirring occasionally, until the flavors combine, 10 minutes. Add the rotisserie chicken, stir to combine and simmer for 5 minutes more. Serve warm and top with any or all of the optional toppings listed.

SERVING SIZE: About 2 cups (500 mL)

TOBY'S TIP: You can use mild or hot chopped green chiles, or get two cans of each for medium-hot chili. Swap the cannellini beans for great Northern beans or pinto beans.

WEEKNIGHT CHICKEN SOFT TACOS

Dinner will be ready in 15 minutes when you use a rotisserie chicken to get these tacos on the table. Seasoned with pantry staples and quickly heated on the stove, they come together in a flash. Taco Tuesday can't get easier than that!

1 tbsp (15 mL) olive oil

4½-oz (127 mL) can chopped green chiles, with juice

4 cups (1 L) shredded rotisserie chicken

2 tsp (10 mL) chili powder

1½ tsp (7 mL) ground cumin

1 tsp (5 mL) paprika

½ tsp (2 mL) garlic powder

½ tsp (2 mL) onion powder

¼ tsp (1 mL) salt

Nonstick cooking spray

Eight 6-inch (15 cm) flour tortillas

TOPPINGS (OPTIONAL)

Chunky Salsa (page 182) or store-bought salsa

Sour cream

Chopped fresh cilantro

Freshly squeezed lime juice

1. In a large skillet, heat the oil over medium heat. When the oil is shimmering, add the green chiles with juice and cook until fragrant, about 2 minutes. Add the chicken, chili powder, cumin, paprika, garlic powder, onion powder and salt and toss to coat. Cook until the chicken is heated through and the flavors combine, 5 minutes. Set aside to slightly cool.

2. Wipe the skillet clean with a paper towel, coat with cooking spray and heat over medium-low heat. Place 1 tortilla in the skillet and heat for 1 minute on each side, until warmed through. Place the warmed tortilla on a plate and cover with a clean cloth or paper towel. Repeat with the remaining tortillas.

3. Place ½ cup (125 mL) of the chicken mixture into a warmed tortilla and top with any or all of the optional toppings listed. Repeat for the remaining tortillas for a total of 8 tacos.

SERVING SIZE: 2 tacos

TOBY'S TIP: Give your tacos a nutritional boot by using whole wheat flour tortillas. You can also lighten up the toppings by using nonfat plain Greek yogurt instead of sour cream.

CHICKEN TACOS
WITH PINEAPPLE SALSA

Tacos made with rotisserie chicken are a simple weeknight meal. Keep it interesting by making your own speedy salsa. Canned pineapple will work, but I prefer fresh for this recipe. You can use leftovers to make Hawaiian Chicken Pizza (page 143) or cut it into chunks and enjoy as a snack or for dessert.

PINEAPPLE SALSA

½ cup (125 mL) finely diced pineapple

⅓ cucumber, finely chopped

¼ cup (60 mL) chopped red onion

1 jalapeño pepper, seeded and finely chopped

2 tbsp (30 mL) chopped fresh cilantro

1 tbsp (15 mL) freshly squeezed lime juice

¼ tsp (1 mL) salt

TACOS

Nonstick cooking spray

Eight 8-inch (20 cm) flour tortillas

4 cups (1 L) shredded rotisserie chicken, warmed

1 avocado, cut into 8 slices

2 limes, quartered

1. **PINEAPPLE SALSA:** In a medium bowl, toss together the pineapple, cucumber, red onion, jalapeño, cilantro, lime juice and salt.

2. **TACOS:** Coat a large skillet with nonstick cooking spray and heat over medium-low heat. Place 1 tortilla in the skillet and heat for 1 minute or each side. Place the warmed tortilla on a plate and cover with a clean cloth or paper towel. Repeat with the remaining tortillas.

3. To assemble the tacos, place 1 warmed tortilla on a large plate. Spoon ½ cup (125 mL) of the chicken into the center of the taco, then top with a slice of avocado and 3 tbsp (45 mL) of the pineapple salsa. Repeat for the remaining tacos. Serve each taco with a lime wedge.

SERVING SIZE: 1 taco

TOBY'S TIPS: Give your tacos a nutritional boost by using whole wheat tortillas.

•

To warm the rotisserie chicken, either reheat the shredded chicken in the microwave or place in a skillet and reheat over medium heat.

CHICKEN BURRITOS

My kids have been my recipe testers for many years, and let me tell you, they're the best judges of how good a recipe is. After these burritos, each of my three kids licked the plate clean, and my son asked for seconds (a rare occurrence!).

1 tbsp (15 mL) olive oil

1 small onion, chopped

1 jalapeño pepper, seeds removed and chopped

1½ cups (375 mL) chopped rotisserie chicken

½ cup (125 mL) canned reduced-sodium black beans, drained and rinsed

½ cup (125 mL) frozen corn kernels, thawed

2 tbsp (30 mL) tomato paste

2 tbsp (30 mL) reduced-sodium ready-to-use chicken broth

1 tsp (5 mL) chili powder

1 tsp (5 mL) ground cumin

Five 10-inch (25 cm) flour tortillas

10 tbsp (150 mL) Mexican blend cheese, divided

10 tbsp (150 mL) Chunky Salsa (page 182) or store-bought salsa, divided

Nonstick cooking spray

TOPPINGS (OPTIONAL)

Chunky Salsa (page 182) or store-bought salsa

Sour cream

Guacamole

1. Heat the oil in a large skillet over medium heat. When the oil is shimmering, add the onion and jalapeño and cook, stirring occasionally, until the vegetables soften, 3 minutes. Add the chicken, black beans, corn, tomato paste, chicken broth, chili powder and cumin and toss to combine. Cook until the chicken is warmed through, stirring occasionally, about 3 minutes.

2. In the center of a tortilla, spoon 2 tbsp (30 mL) each of the cheese and salsa followed by ½ cup (125 mL) of the chicken mixture. Fold the bottom edge of the tortilla up and over the filling, fold in the opposite sides and roll up from the bottom. Place the burrito seam side down and repeat for 4 more burritos.

3. Coat a large skillet with nonstick cooking spray. When the oil is shimmering, add the burrito seam side down and cook for 3 minutes, use a spatula to flip and cook for 3 minutes more on the opposite side. Repeat with the remaining burritos. Serve with salsa, sour cream and guacamole (if using).

SERVING SIZE: 1 burrito

TOBY'S TIP: Give your burritos a nutritional boost by using whole wheat tortillas, and lighten them up by using reduced-fat cheese and topping with nonfat plain Greek yogurt.

CREAMY ARTICHOKE, CHICKEN AND SPINACH PASTA

You don't need cream in order to make a creamy pasta sauce. To achieve a smooth white sauce, this recipe uses a combination of flour, chicken broth and milk. Just be sure to follow the instructions in the method carefully so you don't end up with a lumpy sauce.

10 oz (300 g) medium pasta shells

2 tbsp (30 mL) olive oil or canola oil

1 clove garlic, minced

14-oz (398 mL) can artichoke hearts, drained, rinsed and coarsely chopped

2 cups (500 mL) baby spinach

2 cups (500 mL) shredded rotisserie chicken

2 tbsp (30 mL) all-purpose flour

1 cup (250 mL) reduced-sodium ready-to-use chicken broth

1 cup (250 mL) milk

½ cup (125 mL) freshly grated Parmesan cheese

¼ tsp (1 mL) freshly ground black pepper

¼ tsp (1 mL) hot pepper flakes

1. Bring a 4-quart (4 L) stockpot of water to a boil over high heat. Add the pasta and cook until the pasta is fork-tender, 8 to 9 minutes. Drain and set aside to slightly cool.

2. Heat the oil in a large skillet over medium heat. When the oil is shimmering, add the garlic, artichoke hearts, baby spinach and chicken and stir to combine. Cook until the spinach has wilted, 3 to 4 minutes. Sprinkle the flour over the vegetables, stir in the chicken broth and milk and bring the mixture to a boil over high heat. Lower the heat to medium-low and slowly stir the liquid until it begins to thicken slightly, 3 to 4 minutes. Add the Parmesan cheese, black pepper and pepper flakes and stir to combine.

3. Add the cooked shells to the cream sauce and toss to combine.

MAKE AHEAD: The pasta shells can be made ahead of time and stored in the refrigerator up to 4 days. Warm the pasta shells before adding to the sauce.

SERVING SIZE: 1¾ cups (425 mL)

TOBY'S TIP: Give this dish a nutritional boost by using whole wheat pasta shells and lighten it up by using 2% milk.

HERBED CHICKEN MEATBALLS

Making meatballs from rotisserie chicken instead of raw meat means a shorter cook time — a true time-saver. Fresh parsley and basil are classic herbs in Italian-style meatballs, but you can also use mint, rosemary or whatever you have on hand. Enjoy these meatballs tossed in your favorite tomato sauce and served over pasta, spaghetti squash or zucchini noodles.

PREHEAT THE OVEN TO 375°F (190°C)
BLENDER, INSTANT-READ THERMOMETER

Nonstick cooking spray

4 cups (1 L) shredded rotisserie chicken

1 small yellow onion, chopped

1 clove garlic, crushed with a large knife

½ cup (125 mL) coarsely chopped fresh parsley

½ cup (125 mL) coarsely chopped fresh basil

¼ tsp (1 mL) salt

⅛ tsp (0.5 mL) freshly ground black pepper

1 large egg

1. Coat a baking sheet with nonstick cooking spray.

2. Place the chicken, onion, garlic, parsley, basil, salt, pepper and egg in a blender, and blend until almost smooth. Place the mixture in a medium bowl.

3. Form 1 tbsp (15 mL) of the chicken mixture into a ball, and place on the prepared baking sheet. Repeat with the remaining chicken mixture, leaving about 1 inch (2.5 cm) of space between meatballs, to make about 20 meatballs total.

4. Place the baking sheet in the preheated oven and bake until the meatballs are slightly browned and an instant-read thermometer inserted into several meatballs reads 165°F (75°C), 18 to 20 minutes.

MEAL PREP: To freeze, store cooled meatballs in a sealable container in the freezer for up to 2 months. To thaw, refrigerate overnight. Reheat the meatballs in a saucepan along with the sauce of your choice. Bring the mixture to a boil. Reduce the heat and simmer until warmed through, 10 to 15 minutes. Individual servings of meatballs can also be reheated in the microwave on High for 2 minutes.

SERVING SIZE: About 5 meatballs

TOBY'S TIP: Wet your hands so you can more easily work with the chicken mixture and form the meatballs.

THAI CHICKEN TACOS
WITH CARROT-CABBAGE SLAW

The Thai-inspired flavors in these quick tacos will take your Taco Tuesday to the next level. Serve with tortilla chips or cut veggies dipped in guac.

DRESSING

2 cloves garlic, minced

Juice of 1 lime

4 tsp (20 mL) fish sauce (nam pla)

4 tsp (20 mL) reduced-sodium soy sauce

1 tbsp (15 mL) water

1 tsp (5 mL) brown sugar

⅛ tsp (0.5 mL) hot pepper flakes

SLAW

2 medium carrots, shredded

4 cups (1 L) shredded napa green cabbage

½ cup (125 mL) chopped fresh cilantro

TACOS

Nonstick cooking spray

Eight 6-inch (15 cm) flour tortillas

1 tbsp (15 mL) olive oil or canola oil

2 cups (500 mL) shredded rotisserie chicken

1 lime, quartered

1. **DRESSING:** In a small mixing bowl, whisk together the garlic, lime juice, fish sauce, soy sauce, water, brown sugar and pepper flakes.

2. **SLAW:** In a large mixing bowl, toss together the carrots, cabbage and cilantro. Add 3 tbsp (45 mL) of the dressing and toss to combine.

3. **TACOS:** Coat a large skillet with cooking spray and heat over medium-low heat. Place 1 tortilla in the skillet and heat for 1 minute on each side, until warmed through. Place on a plate and cover with a clean cloth or paper towel. Repeat for the remaining tortillas.

4. Heat the oil in the same large skillet over medium heat. When the oil is shimmering, add the chicken and the remaining dressing and toss to evenly coat. Heat the chicken through, about 3 minutes.

5. In each tortilla, place ¼ cup (60 mL) of the slaw and top with ¼ cup (60 mL) of the chicken. Serve with extra slaw on the side and a wedge of lime.

MAKE AHEAD: Make the slaw the night before. It tastes even better if the flavors can marinate for at least 30 minutes and up to 24 hours.

SERVING SIZE: 2 tacos, plus ½ cup (125 mL) slaw

CHICKEN AND VEGETABLE STIR-FRY

Loaded with succulent chicken and fresh broccoli, cauliflower and carrots, this stir-fry is an easy go-to weeknight dinner. The ingredients to make the sauce are stored in your pantry, so all you need to pick up from the store is the rotisserie chicken and vegetables. It really can't get much easier than that!

⅓ cup (75 mL) reduced-sodium ready-to-use chicken or vegetable broth

1½ tbsp (22 mL) soy sauce

1 tbsp (15 mL) toasted sesame oil

1 tbsp (15 mL) cornstarch

¼ tsp (1 mL) ground ginger

1 tsp (5 mL) Thai chile sauce (such as Sriracha)

1 tbsp (15 mL) olive oil or canola oil

2 cups (500 mL) broccoli florets

2 cups (500 mL) cauliflower florets

2 carrots, cut into ¼-inch (1 cm) rounds

3 cups (750 mL) shredded rotisserie chicken

1. In a medium bowl, whisk together the broth, soy sauce, sesame oil, cornstarch, ginger and Thai chile sauce.

2. In a large wok or skillet over medium-high heat, heat the oil until it shimmers. Add the broccoli, cauliflower and carrots and cook until the vegetables begin to soften, about 5 minutes, stirring occasionally. Add the chicken and continue cooking, stirring occasionally, until the chicken is heated through, an additional 3 to 4 minutes. Add the sauce to the stir-fry and cook, stirring frequently, until the sauce begins to thicken, about 2 minutes.

SERVING SIZE: 1½ cups (375 mL)

TOBY'S TIPS: To cut back on salt, use reduced-sodium soy sauce.

To help minimize food waste in your home, use leftover veggies (cooked, fresh, frozen or canned), such as asparagus, spinach, zucchini and peppers.

CASHEW CHICKEN

There's no need to order in Chinese food when you can make your own Cashew Chicken in less time than it would take to get delivery. This quick stir-fry will keep you full because cashews are packed with heart-healthy unsaturated fat, which takes longer to digest and keeps you feeling satisfied.

¼ cup (60 mL) reduced-sodium ready-to-use chicken broth

2 tbsp (30 mL) soy sauce

1½ tbsp (22 mL) oyster sauce

1 tbsp (15 mL) unseasoned rice vinegar

2 tsp (10 mL) pure maple syrup

1 tsp (5 mL) toasted sesame oil

1 tbsp (15 mL) cornstarch

4 oz (125 g) raw, unsalted cashews

1 tbsp (15 mL) olive oil or canola oil

1 clove garlic, minced

1 red bell pepper, sliced into 1-inch (2.5 cm) strips

2 cups (500 mL) broccoli florets

4 cups (1 L) shredded rotisserie chicken

1. In a small bowl, whisk together the chicken broth, soy sauce, oyster sauce, rice vinegar, maple syrup and sesame oil. Whisk in the cornstarch and set aside.

2. Place the cashews in a small skillet over low heat. Toast until the cashews are fragrant, 2 to 3 minutes, being careful not to burn the cashews. Remove the cashews from the pan and place in a clean bowl. Set aside to slightly cool.

3. In a large wok or skillet, heat the oil over medium-high heat. When the oil is shimmering, add the garlic, red pepper, broccoli and chicken and cook until slightly softened, about 3 minutes. Add the toasted cashews and cook until heated through, about 2 minutes. Add the sauce and stir until the sauce thickens, about 2 minutes. Serve warm.

SERVING SIZE: 1½ cups (375 mL)

TOBY'S TIPS: Lighten up this dish by using reduced-sodium soy sauce.

• You can serve the stir-fry over white rice, or give the dish a nutritional boost by using brown rice, quinoa, farro or whole wheat pasta.

CHICKEN, SPINACH AND TOMATO OVEN QUESADILLAS

Quesadillas are a quick and versatile dish—perfect for when you're crunched for time. You can make them one at a time on the stove, but if you're cooking for a group, you can make a batch in the oven instead.

PREHEAT THE OVEN TO 350°F (180°C)

Nonstick cooking spray

Eight 8-inch (20 cm) flour tortillas

1 cup (250 mL) packed baby spinach

2 cups (500 mL) shredded rotisserie chicken

2 plum (Roma) tomatoes, thinly sliced

1⅓ cups (330mL) shredded Mexican blend cheese

TOPPINGS (OPTIONAL)

Chunky Salsa (page 182) or store-bought salsa

Guacamole

Sour cream

1. Coat two baking sheets with nonstick cooking spray.

2. Coat one side of 4 tortillas with cooking spray, and place 2 of the tortillas coated side down onto each baking sheet. Divide the spinach and chicken evenly among the 4 tortillas. Top each tortilla with about 4 tomato slices, sprinkle each tortilla with ⅓ cup (75 mL) of the cheese, and then top with a tortilla. Use clean hands to gently press down on the quesadilla.

3. Bake in the preheated oven for 8 minutes, until the cheese has melted and the tortillas are slightly browned. Remove the baking sheets from the oven and let the tortillas cool for 5 minutes before slicing each quesadilla into quarters. Serve with your choice of toppings (if using).

SERVING SIZE: 1 quesadilla

TOBY'S TIP: Give these quesadillas a nutritional boost by using whole wheat tortillas and lighten up the dish by using shredded reduced-fat Mexican blend cheese and nonfat Greek yogurt instead of sour cream for topping, if using.

SPICY PEACH AND CHICKEN OVEN QUESADILLAS

Peaches and jalapeños make a sweet, tart and spicy combination that is balanced beautifully with rotisserie chicken. If you're looking to add even more spiciness, opt for pepper Jack cheese.

PREHEAT THE OVEN TO 350°F (OR 180°C)

Nonstick cooking spray

Eight 8-inch (20 cm) flour tortillas, preferably whole wheat

2 cups (500 mL) shredded rotisserie chicken

2 cups (500 mL) fresh or frozen and thawed sliced peaches

2 jalapeño peppers, seeds and ribs removed and thinly sliced

2 cups (500 mL) shredded Monterey Jack cheese

¼ cup (60 mL) chopped fresh cilantro

TOPPINGS (OPTIONAL)

Chunky Salsa (page 182) or store-bought salsa

Sour cream

1. Coat two baking sheets with nonstick cooking spray.

2. Coat one side of 4 tortillas with cooking spray, and place 2 of the tortillas coated side down onto each baking sheet. Divide the chicken and peaches evenly among the 4 tortillas, spreading the chicken to the edge of the tortilla. Scatter the jalapeños over the chicken and then sprinkle each tortilla with ½ cup (125 mL) of the cheese and 1 tbsp (15 mL) of the cilantro. Top with the remaining tortillas and use clean hands to gently press down on the quesadillas.

3. Bake in the preheated oven for 8 minutes, until the cheese has melted and the tortillas are slightly browned. Remove the baking sheets from the oven and let cool for 5 minutes before slicing each quesadilla into quarters. Serve with salsa or sour cream, if using.

SERVING SIZE: 1 quesadilla

TOBY'S TIP: Give this dish a nutritional boost by using whole wheat tortillas, and lighten it up by using shredded reduced-fat cheese and serve with nonfat plain Greek yogurt.

HAWAIIAN CHICKEN PIZZA

Use leftover rotisserie chicken to build this yummy pizza with extra protein. This Hawaiian-inspired pizza combines pineapple, rotisserie chicken and barbecue sauce — but you can make a chicken and vegetable or just good old tomato sauce with cheese topped with chicken.

PREHEAT THE OVEN TO 375°F (180°C)

Nonstick cooking spray

1½ cups (375 mL) shredded rotisserie chicken

¾ cup (175 mL) Homemade Barbecue Sauce (page 178) or store-bought barbecue sauce

10-oz (300 g) ready-made pizza crust

1 cup (250 mL) canned or jarred tomato sauce

2 cups (500 mL) shredded mozzarella cheese

1 cup (250 mL) finely chopped fresh pineapple or canned pineapple tidbits packed in 100% juice

1. Coat a pizza pan or baking sheet with cooking spray.

2. In a medium bowl, add the rotisserie chicken and barbecue sauce. Toss to combine.

3. Place the pizza crust on the pan and evenly spread the tomato sauce over the crust. Sprinkle evenly with the cheese. Top evenly with the rotisserie chicken mixture and pineapple.

4. Bake in the preheated oven until the crust is crisp and browned around the edges, 10 minutes. Let the pizza cool for 10 minutes before cutting into eight even slices.

SERVING SIZE: 2 slices

TOBY'S TIPS: To give this pizza a nutritional boost, use whole wheat pizza crust and lighten it up by using shredded part-skim mozzarella cheese.

•

Some store-bought barbecue sauces contain a lot of added sugar. To avoid eating a lot of hidden sugar, check the ingredient list and nutrition label to select one with the least amount of added sugar, or you can make your own Homemade Barbecue Sauce (page 178).

CHICKEN, AVOCADO AND STRAWBERRY FLATBREAD

This summertime flatbread combines sweet strawberries with creamy avocado and ricotta cheese, topped with shredded rotisserie chicken, and is then quickly warmed in the oven and finished with a simple balsamic sauce. You can also make a flatbread using mozzarella with fresh tomato and basil and top it with a drizzle of the same balsamic sauce.

PREHEAT THE OVEN TO 375°F (180°C)

Nonstick cooking spray

¼ cup (60 mL) balsamic vinegar

2 tsp (10 mL) honey

Two 4.5-oz (130 g) pieces naan bread

1 cup (250 mL) ricotta cheese

1 cup (250 mL) shredded rotisserie chicken

1 avocado, thinly sliced

1 cup (250 mL) sliced strawberries

2 tbsp (30 mL) fresh basil, sliced into ribbons

1. Coat a baking sheet with nonstick cooking spray.

2. In a small saucepan, bring the vinegar and honey to a boil. Reduce the heat to low and simmer, whisking regularly, until the liquid is reduced by half and is thick enough to coat the back of a spoon, about 5 minutes. Set aside and let cool slightly.

3. Place the naan bread onto the prepared baking sheet. Use the back of a spoon or spatula to spread the ricotta cheese evenly over the breads. Top with the chicken, avocado and strawberries. Bake in the preheated oven for 10 minutes, until the chicken is warmed through. Remove and let cool slightly before drizzling with the reduced balsamic vinegar and sprinkling with the basil.

4. To serve, slice each naan bread in half. Serve warm.

SERVING SIZE: ½ flatbread

TOBY'S TIP: Give this flatbread a nutritional boost by using whole-grain naan (I like Stonefire brand), and lighten it up by using part-skim ricotta cheese.

CHICKEN WITH CARAMELIZED ONIONS

You can bring out the sweetness of onions by adding a touch of brown sugar. This quickly releases the natural sugars, resulting in an intense, delicious flavor. When combined with moist rotisserie chicken, it makes a mouthwatering dinner that can be whipped up in less than 30 minutes.

1 cup (250 mL) reduced-sodium ready-to-use chicken broth

1 clove garlic, minced

¼ cup (60 mL) unseasoned rice vinegar

¼ cup (60 mL) soy sauce

3 tbsp (45 mL) light brown sugar

¼ tsp (1 mL) ground ginger

2 tbsp (30 mL) olive oil or canola oil

1 tbsp (15 mL) unsalted butter

3 large yellow onions, thinly sliced

4 cups (1 L) shredded rotisserie chicken

1. In a small bowl, whisk together the chicken broth, garlic, rice vinegar, soy sauce, brown sugar and ginger.

2. In a large skillet, heat the oil and butter over medium heat. Add the onions and cook over medium-low heat, uncovered, until slightly softened, about 8 minutes, stirring occasionally.

3. Add the broth mixture and chicken to the skillet and raise the heat to high. Bring the mixture to a boil, and then lower the heat to medium. Cook, stirring occasionally, until the chicken is heated through, about 5 minutes.

SERVING SIZE: 1½ cups (375 mL)

TOBY'S TIPS: Lessen the salt in this dish by using reduced-sodium soy sauce.

•

Serve with Sheet Pan Vegetables (page 160), Honey Roasted Carrots (page 158) or Brown Rice with Peas and Carrots (page 165).

LEMON AND GARLIC SKILLET CHICKEN

Fresh lemons, garlic and onions are staples in my kitchen, especially because they last a while. I recommend always keeping them on hand. That way you can whip up recipes like this one, where the only ingredient you'll need from the store is the rotisserie chicken.

½ cup (125 mL) white cooking wine or dry white wine

Juice of 1 lemon

1 tsp (5 mL) dried thyme

1 tsp (5 mL) dried parsley

½ tsp (2 mL) dried rosemary

¼ tsp (1 mL) salt

¼ tsp (1 mL) freshly ground black pepper

⅛ tsp (0.5 mL) hot pepper flakes

1 tbsp (15 mL) olive oil

1 medium onion, finely chopped

3 cloves garlic, minced

4 cups (1 L) shredded rotisserie chicken

1. In a small bowl, whisk together the wine, lemon juice, thyme, parsley, rosemary, salt, pepper and pepper flakes.

2. Heat the oil in a large skillet over medium heat. When the oil is shimmering, add the onion and garlic and cook, stirring occasionally, until the onion is soft and translucent and the garlic is fragrant, about 3 minutes. Add the shredded chicken and toss to combine. Add the wine mixture and bring to a boil, lower the heat to medium-low and cook until the chicken is heated through, 5 to 6 minutes.

SERVING SIZE: 1 cup (250 mL)

TOBY'S TIP: When was the last time you cleaned out your spices? The recommended shelf life is between 2 and 3 years. If you have spices sitting in your pantry longer than that, it's time to toss them.

CHICKEN AND COUSCOUS

Made from a combination of semolina wheat and water, couscous has a taste similar to pasta. There are several types of couscous, including the small Moroccan couscous (used in this recipe), which is about three times the size of cornmeal. You can also find larger grained couscous called Israeli or pearled couscous.

COUSCOUS

1¼ cups (300 mL) reduced-sodium ready-to-use chicken or vegetable broth

1 tbsp (15 mL) unsalted butter

Rind of 1 lemon

1 cup (250 mL) frozen peas

1 carrot, shredded

½ cup (125 mL) couscous

CHICKEN

1 tbsp (15 mL) olive oil

1 medium onion, chopped

2 cloves garlic, minced

2 cups (500 mL) store-bought marinara sauce

4 cups (1 L) shredded rotisserie chicken

1. **COUSCOUS:** In a medium saucepan, add the broth, butter and lemon rind and bring to a boil. Add the peas and carrot, lower the heat to medium and cook, stirring occasionally, for 5 minutes. Stir in the couscous and cover. Remove the saucepan from the heat and let stand for 5 minutes. Uncover and fluff with a fork. Remove and discard the lemon rind.

2. **CHICKEN:** In a large skillet, heat the oil. When the oil is shimmering, add the onion and garlic and cook until the onion is soft and translucent and the garlic is fragrant, 3 minutes. Add the tomato sauce and bring the mixture to a boil. Lower the heat to medium, add the chicken and toss with the tomato sauce to combine. Continue cooking until the chicken is heated through, about 5 minutes. Serve with the couscous.

SERVING SIZE: 1 cup (250 mL) chicken, plus ¾ cup (175 mL) couscous

TOBY'S TIPS: For a nutritional boost, use the whole wheat variety of couscous, or swap the couscous for brown rice with the same ratio of rice to chicken broth as listed in the recipe above.

Both Moroccan couscous and the larger Israeli or pearled couscous are available in whole wheat varieties, which will contain 5 to 6 grams of fiber per 1 cup (250 mL) serving.

STOVETOP CHICKEN AND CAULIFLOWER RICE

You can make your own cauliflower rice from fresh cauliflower, or make it simple by picking up a bag in the frozen aisle in your grocery — right next to the frozen vegetables. I prefer to buy it already riced and frozen, but the choice is yours! See Toby's Tip for advice on thawing frozen cauliflower rice.

1 tbsp (15 mL) olive oil

1 shallot, chopped

1 clove garlic, minced

2 carrots, shredded

1 cup (250 mL) reduced-sodium ready-to-use chicken broth or vegetable broth

Grated zest of 1 lemon

Juice of 1 lemon

1 tsp (5 mL) oregano

¼ tsp (1 mL) salt

⅛ tsp (0.5 mL) freshly ground black pepper

10-oz (300g) bag frozen riced cauliflower, thawed

2 cups (500 mL) shredded rotisserie chicken

1. In a large skillet, heat the oil over medium heat. When the oil is shimmering, add the shallot, garlic and carrots and cook, stirring occasionally, until the vegetables soften, about 3 minutes. Add the broth, lemon zest, lemon juice, oregano, salt and pepper and bring to a boil over high heat. Add the riced cauliflower and chicken and stir to evenly coat. Raise the temperature to high and bring the mixture to a boil. Reduce the heat to medium-low, cover and cook until the cauliflower is heated through, about 10 minutes. Serve warm.

SERVING SIZE: 1¾ cups (425 mL)

TOBY'S TIP: Without proper thawing and draining of the frozen riced cauliflower, the dish will end up too watery. Thaw the frozen cauliflower at room temperature in a fine-mesh strainer to remove excess water. Once the riced cauliflower has thawed for about 30 minutes, press it into the colander with a clean paper towel to drain even more water.

DRIED FRUIT AND CHICKEN SKILLET

Plumped dried fruit is the star of the sauce in this chicken skillet. The dish gets its sweetness from dried fruit and pure maple syrup, and warm, fragrant spices add depth and complexity. It's a spin on a dish my mom used to make, and to this day it has a warming place in my heart. Serve the sweet and savory chicken over white rice or quinoa.

¾ cup (175 mL) prunes

¾ cup (175 mL) dried apricots

1½ cups (375 mL) hot water

¼ cup (60 mL) pure maple syrup

1 tsp (5 mL) grated orange zest

¼ tsp (1 mL) ground cinnamon

⅛ tsp (0.5 mL) ground nutmeg

4 cups (1 L) shredded rotisserie chicken

1. In a medium heatproof bowl, add the prunes and apricots and cover with the hot water. Allow the fruit to soak for 15 minutes.

2. In a large skillet, add the water with fruit, maple syrup, orange zest, cinnamon and nutmeg; stir to combine, and bring to a boil over high heat. Add the chicken and coat with the sauce. Raise the heat to high and bring the mixture to a boil. Lower the heat to medium and cook, covered, until the chicken is heated through, 5 to 8 minutes.

SERVING SIZE: About 1 cup (250 mL)

TOBY'S TIP: Mix and match your favorite flavors. Swap the same amounts of raisins, dried cranberries or tart cherries for the prunes and apricots.

CREOLE CHICKEN OVER GRITS

Grits are a creamy porridge made from ground dried hominy and water or broth. The traditional method requires patience and slow cooking because the grits need to fully absorb the liquid in order to bring out the flavor and sweetness of the corn. Here I've called for the quick-cooking variety to get dinner on the table faster.

2¼ cups (560 mL) water, divided

½ cup (125 mL) quick-cooking grits or polenta

⅛ tsp (0.5 mL) salt

1 tbsp (15 mL) olive oil

3 cloves garlic, minced

2 cups (500 mL) reduced-sodium ready-to-use chicken broth

1 tsp (5 mL) Creole seasoning

2 tbsp (30 mL) cornstarch

4 cups (1 L) shredded rotisserie chicken

1. In a small saucepan, bring 2 cups (500 mL) of the water to a boil. Stir constantly while adding the grits and salt. Reduce the heat to low and simmer, covered, for about 7 minutes or until cooked through. Set aside to slightly cool.

2. Heat the oil in a large skillet over medium heat. When the oil is shimmering, add the garlic and cook until fragrant, 1 minute. Add the broth and Creole seasoning, and bring to a boil. In a small bowl, whisk the cornstarch with the remaining water. Add the cornstarch mixture to the skillet and cook, stirring constantly, until the sauce thickens, about 2 minutes. Add the chicken to the skillet and cook until heated through, 7 to 8 minutes.

3. Serve the chicken warm, ladled over the grits.

SERVING SIZE: 1 cup (250 mL) chicken and about ½ cup (125 mL) grits

TOBY'S TIPS: If you like your Creole chicken really spicy, then add the Creole seasoning in increments of ½ tsp (2 mL) until you reach your desired heat level.

•

For even more flavor, mix in shredded cheese when you remove the grits from the heat.

SPANISH-STYLE CHICKEN WITH PEPPERS AND OLIVES

Mediterranean dishes tend to be filled with vegetables, lean protein and healthy fats (hello, olives!), and this meal is no exception. Loaded with bell peppers, mushrooms and tomatoes, this dish is heavy on vegetables and accented with kalamata olives and creamy crumbled goat cheese.

2 tbsp (30 mL) olive oil or canola oil

1 large onion, thinly sliced

1 clove garlic, minced

1 green bell pepper, seeded and cut into ¼-inch (0.5 cm) strips

1 yellow bell pepper, seeded and cut into ¼-inch (0.5 cm) strips

8 oz (227 g) white mushrooms, thinly sliced

4 cups (1 L) shredded rotisserie chicken

28-oz (796 mL) can crushed tomatoes, with juice

⅓ cup (75 mL) halved and pitted kalamata olives

1 tsp (5 mL) dried parsley

¼ tsp (1 mL) salt

¼ tsp (1 mL) freshly ground black pepper

⅓ cup (75 mL) crumbled goat cheese

1. Heat the oil in a large skillet over medium heat. When the oil is shimmering, add the onion and garlic and cook, stirring occasionally, until the onion is translucent and the garlic is fragrant, 2 minutes. Add the green and yellow peppers and mushrooms and cook, stirring occasionally, until the vegetables begin to soften, about 8 minutes.

2. Add the chicken, tomatoes with juice, olives, parsley flakes, salt and black pepper and toss to combine. Raise the heat to high and bring the mixture to a boil. Reduce the heat to medium-low and simmer, covered, for 10 minutes until the chicken is heated through and the flavors combine.

3. Remove the skillet from the heat. Sprinkle with the crumbled goat cheese before serving.

SERVING SIZE: 2 cups (500 mL)

TOBY'S TIP: Reduce the salt in this recipe by omitting the kalamata olives or goat cheese, or both.

POMEGRANATE CHICKEN

Pomegranate juice adds a sweet and tart flavor to this dish. It's jam-packed with polyphenols, which are antioxidants linked to preventing heart disease and cancer. One study published in the *Journal of Biomedical Biotechnology* determined that pomegranate juice has three times more polyphenols than green tea and red wine — just another reason to add pomegranate juice to your dishes!

1½ cups (375 mL) 100% pomegranate juice

3 tbsp (45 mL) honey

⅓ cup (75 mL) balsamic vinegar

4 cups (1 L) shredded rotisserie chicken

1 tbsp (15 mL) chopped fresh rosemary leaves

½ cup (125 mL) pomegranate arils

1. In a medium bowl, whisk together the pomegranate juice, honey and vinegar. Place the mixture in a large skillet and bring to a boil over medium-high heat. Reduce the heat to medium-low and continue cooking until the sauce is reduced by half, about 5 minutes.

2. Add the rotisserie chicken and rosemary and toss with the pomegranate sauce. Continue cooking over medium heat, covered, until the chicken is heated through, about 5 minutes. Stir in the pomegranate arils. Serve warm.

SERVING SIZE: 1 cup (250 mL)

TOBY'S TIP: If you only have dried rosemary, substitute 1 tsp (5 mL) dried for 1 tbsp (15 mL) rosemary leaves.

CHICKEN IN ORANGE SAUCE

This mouthwatering dish combines the delicious sweetness of orange juice with tangy Asian-inspired flavors for a dinner that's ready in less than 30 minutes. Serve over rice or quinoa.

1 cup (250 mL) orange juice	¼ tsp (1 mL) ground ginger
Grated zest of 1 orange	¼ tsp (1 mL) garlic powder
¼ cup (60 mL) pure maple syrup	1 tbsp (15 mL) cornstarch
2 tbsp (30 mL) unseasoned rice vinegar	4 cups (1 L) shredded rotisserie chicken
2 tbsp (30 mL) soy sauce	2 green onions, green parts only, chopped
1 tsp (5 mL) Thai chile sauce (such as Sriracha)	

1. In a medium bowl, whisk together the orange juice and zest, maple syrup, vinegar, soy sauce, Thai chile sauce, ginger and garlic powder. Add the cornstarch and whisk to incorporate.

2. Heat a large skillet over medium heat. Add the chicken and heat through, about 5 minutes. Add the orange sauce, raise the heat to high and bring the mixture to a boil. Reduce the heat to medium and continue cooking until the sauce thickens, about 2 minutes, stirring occasionally. Remove the skillet from the heat and sprinkle with the green onions before serving.

SERVING SIZE: 1 cup (250 mL)

TOBY'S TIP: Lessen the salt by using reduced-sodium soy sauce.

• Use 100% orange juice in this recipe or freshly squeeze your own to avoid unnecessary added sugar.

SKILLET BALSAMIC CHICKEN

Balsamic vinegar has a strong, delicious flavor that is balanced in this dish with the sweetness of honey (just a touch!) and complements chicken beautifully. Combined with fresh garlic and seasoned with thyme and bay leaves, this flavorful dish is most certainly a crowd-pleaser.

½ cup (125 mL) reduced-sodium ready-to-use chicken broth

⅓ cup (75 mL) balsamic vinegar

1 tbsp (15 mL) honey

½ tsp (2 mL) dried thyme

1 tbsp (15 mL) olive oil or canola oil

2 cloves garlic, minced

2 bay leaves

4 cups (1 L) shredded rotisserie chicken

¼ tsp (1 mL) salt

⅛ tsp (0.5 mL) freshly ground black pepper

1. In a small bowl, whisk together the chicken broth, vinegar, honey and thyme.

2. Heat the oil is a large skillet over medium heat. When the oil is shimmering, add the garlic and cook, stirring occasionally, until fragrant, 30 seconds. Add the broth mixture and bay leaves, raise the heat to high and bring to a boil. Reduce the heat to medium-low and simmer until the mixture is reduced by half, stirring occasionally, 3 to 5 minutes. Add the rotisserie chicken, salt and pepper and toss with the sauce. Raise the heat to medium and continue cooking, stirring occasionally, uncovered, until the chicken is heated through, about 5 minutes.

SERVING SIZE: 1 cup (250 mL)

TOBY'S TIP: Play with your salt and pepper. If you need a little extra sprinkle of salt or freshly ground black pepper, wait until the dish is finished and give it a taste. Then decide how much you need to add.

MOROCCAN CHICKEN BURGERS

Punch up the flavor of chicken burgers with Moroccan spices like harissa, cumin, ginger and paprika. Toss all the ingredients in the blender, form into patties and cook on the stove — it can't get much easier!

BLENDER, GRILL PAN (OPTIONAL), INSTANT-READ THERMOMETER

SAUCE

1 cup (250 mL) plain yogurt

¼ cup (60 mL) chopped fresh mint or 2 tbsp (30 mL) dried mint

1 tsp (5 mL) garlic powder

¼ tsp (1 mL) salt

BURGERS

2 cups (500 mL) shredded rotisserie chicken

¼ cup (60 mL) unbleached all-purpose flour

1 large egg, beaten

1 tbsp (15 mL) onion powder

1 tbsp (15 mL) harissa

1 tbsp (15 mL) garlic powder

1 tsp (5 mL) paprika

1 tsp (5 mL) ground cumin

½ tsp (2 mL) ground ginger

¼ tsp (1 mL) salt

⅛ tsp (0.5 mL) freshly ground black pepper

Nonstick cooking spray

1 plum (Roma) tomato, thinly sliced

8 leaves lettuce

4 hamburger buns

1. **SAUCE:** Combine the yogurt, mint, garlic powder and salt in a medium bowl.

2. **BURGERS:** Place the chicken in a blender and pulse a few times. Add the flour, egg, onion powder, harissa, garlic powder, paprika, cumin, ginger, salt and pepper. Pulse a few times, scrape down the sides and pulse again to get a rough but even consistency. Form the burger mixture into four even, thin patties.

3. Coat a grill pan or large skillet with nonstick cooking spray. When the oil is shimmering, place the patties about 1 inch (2.5 cm) apart and cook until the burgers reach an internal temperature of 165°F (75°C) when tested with an instant-read thermometer, 4 minutes on each side.

4. To assemble the burgers, place 2 tomato slices and 2 lettuce leaves on the bottom half of each hamburger bun. Add a burger patty and top with ¼ cup (60 mL) of the yogurt sauce and the top half of the bun. Serve warm.

SERVING SIZE: 1 burger

CHAPTER 9

EVERYDAY SIDES

HONEY ROASTED CARROTS

Vegetable side dishes don't have to be complicated or have a long list of ingredients. The baby carrots needed for this recipe require no prep. Just toss them with honey, parsley and olive oil, and they're ready for the oven. It really doesn't get easier than that!

PREHEAT THE OVEN TO 400°F (200°C)

Nonstick cooking spray

2 tbsp (30 mL) olive oil or canola oil

2 tbsp (30 mL) honey

1 tsp (5 mL) dried parsley

1 lb (500 g) baby carrots

1. Coat a baking sheet with nonstick cooking spray.

2. In a large bowl, whisk together the oil, honey and parsley. Add the carrots and toss to coat.

3. Place the carrots in a single layer on the prepared sheet pan. Roast in the preheated oven until softened and slightly browned, 25 to 30 minutes.

SERVING SIZE: ¾ cup (175 mL)

TOBY'S TIP: Serve with the Cashew Chicken (page 139) or Chicken with Caramelized Onions (page 145).

SHEET PAN BROCCOLI AND CAULIFLOWER

Sheet pan recipes are made for weeknights. There is minimal mess, and once you get the sheet pan in the oven there is not much else to do — except wait for your delicious food to be cooked to perfection.

PREHEAT THE OVEN TO 400°F (200°C)

3 tbsp (45 mL) olive oil

4 cloves garlic, thinly sliced

½ tsp (2 mL) salt

¼ tsp (1 mL) freshly ground black pepper

⅛ tsp (0.5 mL) hot pepper flakes

1 head broccoli, cut into florets

1 head cauliflower, cut into florets

1. In a large bowl, whisk together the oil, garlic, salt, black pepper and pepper flakes. Add the broccoli and cauliflower florets and toss to evenly coat.

2. Place the broccoli and cauliflower in a single layer on a sheet pan. Roast in the preheated oven until browned on the edges, 20 to 25 minutes.

SERVING SIZE: About 1 cup (250 mL)

TOBY'S TIP: Get creative with your sheet pan vegetables. Add a sprinkle of freshly grated Parmesan cheese, a squeeze of lemon juice or a handful of toasted pine nuts to your vegetables after they come out of the oven.

SAUTÉED ZUCCHINI
WITH LEMON AND PINE NUTS

This simple side has a clean lemon flavor that goes with many dishes in this cookbook, like the Skillet Balsamic Chicken (page 154) or Stovetop Chicken and Cauliflower Rice (page 148). You can also serve it on the side of rotisserie chicken right off the bone. It will make a wonderful addition to your side dish repertoire.

3 tbsp (45 mL) pine nuts

2 tbsp (30 mL) olive oil or canola oil

1 clove garlic, minced

3 medium zucchini, sliced into 1-inch (2.5 cm) rounds

½ tsp (2 mL) salt

¼ tsp (1 mL) freshly ground black pepper

Juice of 1 lemon

1. Place the pine nuts in a medium skillet over medium-low heat. Toast the pine nuts, stirring regularly, until slightly browned, 3 minutes. Spoon the pine nuts into a small bowl; set aside to slightly cool.

2. Heat the oil in the same skillet over medium heat. When the oil is shimmering, add the garlic and cook until fragrant, 30 seconds. Add the zucchini and cook until slightly softened, 10 minutes. Add the salt, pepper and lemon juice and toss to combine.

3. Place the zucchini in a serving dish and sprinkle with the toasted pine nuts. Serve warm.

MAKE AHEAD: Toast the pine nuts up to 1 week in advance and store in a sealed container in a cool, dry place until ready to use.

SERVING SIZE: ¾ cup (175 mL)

TOBY'S TIP: Swap the zucchini for yellow squash or use a combination of both to add color.

GARLIC SAUTÉED SPINACH

Garlic not only adds an aromatic flavor to dishes, but it also comes with an array of good-for-you nutrients. One clove of garlic contains calcium and several B vitamins. Garlic also has the plant chemical allicin, shown to have antibacterial properties.

2 tbsp (30 mL) olive oil or canola oil

3 cloves garlic, minced

10-oz (300 g) package frozen chopped spinach, thawed and well drained

¼ tsp (1 mL) salt

⅛ tsp (0.5 mL) freshly ground black pepper

1. Heat the oil in a large skillet over medium heat. When the oil is shimmering, add the garlic and cook until fragrant, 30 seconds. Add the spinach and cook until warmed through, 5 minutes. Sprinkle with the salt and pepper and toss to combine.

SERVING SIZE: About ½ cup (125 mL)

TOBY'S TIP: Remember to drain your thawed spinach before cooking. This will prevent the spinach from becoming wet and soggy.

ISRAELI COUSCOUS AND MUSHROOMS

Couscous isn't a grain but rather a combination of semolina wheat and water, which makes it more like pasta. There are several types of couscous, including small Moroccan couscous (about three times the size of cornmeal) and the large Israeli couscous (also called pearled couscous). The Chicken and Couscous (page 147) uses the Moroccan couscous, which cooks up in 5 minutes, while this recipe uses the Israeli type, which takes less than 10 minutes to cook.

1 tbsp (15 mL) olive oil or canola oil

1 onion, chopped

1 clove garlic, minced

8 oz (250 g) cremini mushrooms, thinly sliced

1 cup (250 mL) Israeli couscous

1¼ cups (300 mL) reduced-sodium ready-to-use vegetable broth

¼ tsp (1 mL) dried dillweed

¼ tsp (1 mL) salt

⅛ tsp (0.5 mL) freshly ground black pepper

1. Heat the oil in a medium skillet over medium heat. When the oil is shimmering, add the onion and garlic and cook, stirring occasionally, until the onion is translucent and the garlic is fragrant, 3 minutes. Add the mushrooms and cook, stirring occasionally, until softened, 5 minutes.

2. Add the couscous, broth, dillweed, salt and pepper and bring the mixture to a boil. Reduce the heat to medium-low, cover and simmer until the couscous is cooked al dente, 8 minutes. Fluff with a fork before serving.

SERVING SIZE: ¾ cup (175 mL)

TOBY'S TIPS: For a nutrient boost, use whole wheat Israeli couscous.

Serve with Pomegranate Chicken (page 152), Dried Fruit and Chicken Skillet (page 149) or Moroccan Chicken Burgers (page 155).

BROWN RICE
WITH PEAS AND CARROTS

Brown rice is considered a whole grain because the bran and germ, which are removed in white rice, are left intact. This means that you get more nutrients like filling fiber, hunger-fighting protein and energy-boosting B vitamins. Brown rice does take longer to cook than some other grains, but it is simple to prepare.

1 tbsp (15 mL) olive oil

1 onion, chopped

2 cloves garlic, minced

2 carrots, shredded

1 cup (250 mL) frozen peas, thawed

1 cup (250 mL) long-grain brown rice

2 cups (500 mL) reduced-sodium ready-to-use vegetable or chicken broth

2 bay leaves

½ tsp (2 mL) salt

¼ tsp (1 mL) freshly ground black pepper

1. Heat the oil in a medium saucepan over medium heat. When the oil is shimmering, add the onion and garlic and cook, stirring occasionally, until the onion is translucent and the garlic is fragrant, 3 minutes. Add the carrots and peas and cook, stirring occasionally, until softened, 5 minutes. Add the rice and cook, stirring occasionally, for 2 to 3 minutes.

2. Add the broth and bay leaves to the saucepan, raise the heat to high and bring to a boil. Lower the heat to medium-low and simmer, covered, stirring occasionally, until the rice is tender, about 40 minutes. Drain any excess water. Transfer the rice to a large bowl, fluff with a fork and stir in the salt and pepper. Remove the bay leaves and discard.

SERVING SIZE: 1 cup (250 mL)

TOBY'S TIP: Bay leaves impart a delicious flavor to dishes but should be added toward the beginning of a recipe so the flavor has time to seep into your dish. Don't forget to discard the leaf before eating.

GARLIC PARMESAN QUINOA

Hard cheese like Parmesan has a strong flavor, but a little goes a long way. This recipe uses ¼ cup (60 mL) of Parmesan cheese, but you can adjust according to your taste preference and use 2 or 3 tbsp (15 to 30 mL) instead.

1 tbsp (15 mL) olive oil

2 cloves garlic, minced

1 cup (250 mL) quinoa

2 cups (500 mL) reduced-sodium ready-to-use vegetable or chicken broth

¼ tsp (1 mL) salt

¼ tsp (1 mL) freshly ground black pepper

¼ cup (60 mL) freshly grated Parmesan cheese

1. Heat the oil in a medium saucepan over medium heat. When the oil is shimmering, add the garlic and cook, stirring occasionally, until fragrant, 30 seconds. Add the quinoa and cook, stirring occasionally, for 1 to 2 minutes.

2. Add the broth to the saucepan, raise the heat to high and bring to a boil. Reduce the heat to low, cover and simmer until all the liquid has been absorbed, 12 to 15 minutes. Add the salt, pepper and Parmesan cheese and stir to combine.

3. Transfer the quinoa to a serving dish and fluff with a fork before serving.

SERVING SIZE: ¾ cup (175 mL)

TOBY'S TIP: Pair with Chicken with Caramelized Onions (page 145), Chicken Loaf (page 119) or Chicken in Orange Sauce (page 153).

CRANBERRY-ALMOND FARRO

Farro is an Italian-born grain that dates back to ancient Rome. It has a nuttier flavor than brown rice and a pleasant, chewy texture. To cook, combine with water or broth and it's ready in about 30 minutes.

⅓ cup (75 mL) raw almonds, thinly sliced

1 tbsp (15 mL) olive oil or canola oil

1 shallot, chopped

1 cup (250 mL) farro

3 cups (750 mL) reduced-sodium ready-to-use vegetable or chicken broth

½ cup (125 mL) dried cranberries

¼ tsp (1 mL) salt

¼ tsp (1 mL) freshly ground black pepper

1. Place the almonds in a small skillet over medium-low heat. Cook, stirring constantly, until the almonds are fragrant and slightly browned, 3 to 4 minutes.

2. Heat the oil in a medium saucepan over medium heat. When the oil is shimmering, add the shallot and cook, stirring occasionally, until soft and translucent, 2 minutes. Add the farro and cook, stirring regularly, for 2 minutes. Add the broth and bring the mixture to a boil. Reduce the heat and simmer until the farro is cooked through, about 30 minutes. Drain any excess liquid.

3. Transfer the farro to a serving dish. Toss with the toasted almonds, cranberries, salt and pepper. Serve warm.

SERVING SIZE: About ¾ cup (175 mL)

TOBY'S TIPS: Swap the dried cranberries for dried tart cherries.

• Purchase whole almonds to chop and slice for recipes, and use the extras to snack on.

CHAPTER 10

DRESSINGS, SAUCES AND CONDIMENTS

BLUE CHEESE DRESSING

This version of the classic dressing swaps part of the mayo for Greek yogurt, which makes it even creamier without making it heavier. Rich and tangy, it's just the thing to top Buffalo Chicken Salad (page 83) or to serve alongside chicken smothered with your favorite Buffalo wing sauce.

BLENDER

½ cup (125 mL) plain Greek yogurt

¼ cup (60 mL) mayonnaise

3 tbsp (45 mL) milk

1½ oz (45 g) crumbled blue cheese

1 tbsp (15 mL) white wine vinegar

1 tbsp (15 mL) freshly squeezed lemon juice

1 tsp (5 mL) garlic powder

¼ tsp (1 mL) salt

⅛ tsp (0.5 mL) freshly ground black pepper

1. In a blender, combine the Greek yogurt, mayonnaise, milk, blue cheese, vinegar, lemon juice, garlic powder, salt and pepper. Blend until smooth.

2. Use immediately or place in a sealable container in the refrigerator for up to 3 days.

   MAKE AHEAD: The dressing can be made up to 3 days in advance and stored in the refrigerator in a covered container.

   SERVING SIZE: 2 tbsp (30 mL)

TOBY'S TIP: Lighten up this dressing by using nonfat plain Greek yogurt, light mayonnaise and nonfat milk.

LEMON-HERB VINAIGRETTE

This light, lemony dressing is flavored with parsley and just a hint of brown sugar to balance the citrusy tartness. The dressing complements the vegetables in a salad, rather than masking them, bringing out their deliciousness.

1 tsp (5 mL) grated lemon zest

Juice of 3 lemons

2 cloves garlic, minced

2 tsp (10 mL) light brown sugar

1 tsp (5 mL) dried parsley

¼ tsp (1 mL) salt

⅛ tsp (0.5 mL) freshly ground black pepper

½ cup (125 mL) extra virgin olive oil

1. In a medium bowl, whisk together the lemon zest, lemon juice, garlic, brown sugar, parsley, salt and pepper. While whisking continuously, slowly drizzle in the oil until combined.

2. Use immediately or place in a sealable container in the fridge for up to 5 days.

   SERVING SIZE: 2 tbsp (30 mL)

TOBY'S TIP: Pair with the Chicken, Kale and White Bean Salad (page 93).

SIMPLE BALSAMIC VINAIGRETTE

While attending New York University for my degree in clinical nutrition and dietetics, I was lucky enough to take several kitchen classes. One of the first recipes I made was a classic balsamic vinaigrette, which was not only super simple to make but also had such versatility on many salads and as a marinade or dip. My version amps up the flavor and still can be used for all those dishes — and so much more!

½ cup (125 mL) balsamic vinegar

2 tsp (10 mL) Dijon mustard

1 tsp (5 mL) honey

1 clove garlic, minced

½ tsp (2 mL) salt

¼ tsp (1 mL) freshly ground black pepper

½ cup (125 mL) extra virgin olive oil

1. In a medium bowl, whisk together the vinegar, Dijon mustard, honey, garlic, salt and pepper. While continuously whisking, slowly drizzle in the oil until combined.

2. Use immediately or place in a sealable container in the refrigerator for up to 5 days.

MAKE AHEAD: Make the balsamic vinaigrette up to 5 days in advance. Store in the refrigerator in a covered container.

SERVING SIZE: 2 tbsp (30 mL)

TOBY'S TIP: Extra virgin olive oil has a low smoke point, so it works better on uncooked dishes like in dressings or drizzled over vegetables. Olive oil has a higher smoke point than extra virgin olive oil and can be used in stovetop dishes.

EASY RANCH DRESSING

If you typically pick up a bottle of this beloved dressing at the grocery, I challenge you to make this version. You'll find it's so easy and tasty that you'll never turn back to the premade version again.

BLENDER

½ cup (125 mL) low-fat buttermilk

6 tbsp (90 mL) plain Greek yogurt

¼ cup (60 mL) mayonnaise

2 tsp (10 mL) dried parsley

1 tsp (5 mL) dried dillweed

1 tsp (5 mL) dried chives

½ tsp (2 mL) garlic powder

Juice of ½ lemon

½ tsp (2 mL) salt

⅛ tsp (0.5 mL) freshly ground black pepper

⅛ tsp (0.5 mL) cayenne pepper

⅛ tsp (0.5 mL) smoked paprika

1. Add the buttermilk, Greek yogurt, mayonnaise, parsley, dillweed, chives, garlic powder, lemon juice, salt, black pepper, cayenne and smoked paprika to a blender and blend until smooth.

2. Place the dressing in a sealable container and refrigerate for 20 minutes to allow the flavors to combine. The dressing can be stored in the refrigerator for up to 5 days.

MAKE AHEAD: Make the dressing up to 5 days in advance and store covered in the refrigerator.

SERVING SIZE: 2 tbsp (30 mL)

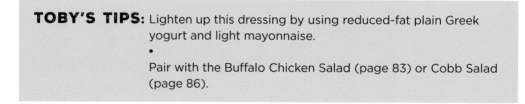

TOBY'S TIPS: Lighten up this dressing by using reduced-fat plain Greek yogurt and light mayonnaise.

•

Pair with the Buffalo Chicken Salad (page 83) or Cobb Salad (page 86).

GINGER DRESSING

With a delicious warm, sweet bite, ginger is the star of this Asian-inspired dressing. Ginger contains several powerful antioxidants that may help fight inflammation. Besides the delicious taste, these are just a few more reasons to enjoy fresh ginger in your meals.

2 tbsp (30 mL) soy sauce

2 tbsp (30 mL) unseasoned rice vinegar

1 tbsp (15 mL) honey

1 tbsp (45 mL) grated gingerroot

1. In a small bowl, whisk together the soy sauce, vinegar, honey and ginger.

2. Use immediately or place the dressing in a sealable container and store in the refrigerator for up to 5 days.

MAKE AHEAD: This dressing can be made up to 5 days in advance and stored in the refrigerator in a covered container.

SERVING SIZE: 2 tbsp (30 mL)

TOBY'S TIPS: Reduce the salt by using reduced-sodium soy sauce.

• Pair with Soba Noodle Salad (page 89).

EASY CAESAR DRESSING

Plain Greek yogurt is my secret to lightening up dressings and dips. It's perfect for adding creaminess without the heaviness that ingredients like mayo or sour cream can impart. This Easy Caesar Dressing uses ready-made staples so you can quickly it whisk together in time for dinner.

¼ cup (60 mL) mayonnaise

½ cup (125 mL) plain Greek yogurt

Juice of 1 lemon

1 tbsp (15 mL) Dijon mustard

1 tsp (5 mL) Worcestershire sauce

¼ cup (60 mL) freshly grated Parmesan cheese

2 cloves garlic, minced

⅛ tsp (0.5 mL) freshly ground black pepper

1. In a small bowl, whisk together the mayonnaise, Greek yogurt, lemon juice, Dijon mustard, Worcestershire sauce, Parmesan cheese, garlic and pepper. Cover and refrigerate for at least 20 minutes to allow the flavors to combine before serving.

2. Use immediately or place in a sealable container in the fridge for up to 3 days.

SERVING SIZE: 2 tbsp (30 mL)

TOBY'S TIPS: Lighten up this dressing by using light mayonnaise and nonfat plain Greek yogurt.

- This version is free of fish. For a more traditional version, add 1 to 2 tsp (5 to 10 mL) anchovy paste.

EASY PESTO SAUCE

Traditional pesto is made using basil, but this pesto uses a combination of basil and spinach, adding even more flavor and nutrition to your sauce.

BLENDER

2 cups (500 mL) fresh basil

1 cup (250 mL) fresh spinach

⅓ cup (75 mL) extra virgin olive oil

1 oz (30 g) pine nuts

2 tbsp (30 mL) freshly grated Parmesan cheese

3 cloves garlic, crushed

⅛ tsp (0.5 mL) salt

1. In a blender, add the basil, spinach, oil, pine nuts, Parmesan cheese, garlic and salt; purée until smooth. Serve immediately or store in a sealable container in the refrigerator for up to 1 week.

SERVING SIZE: 2 tbsp (30 mL)

TOBY'S TIP: Use this pesto for Pesto Pasta with Chicken (page 126), or as a spread for a rotisserie sandwich or panini.

HOMEMADE BARBECUE SAUCE

Pomegranate juice adds a sweet and tart flavor to this barbecue sauce, while the blackstrap molasses adds sweetness. Blackstrap molasses is made when sugar cane is mashed and boiled three times to create a dark, viscous liquid. It has a lower sugar content than sugar cane and small amounts of vitamins and minerals like iron, calcium, magnesium, selenium and vitamin B_6.

½ cup (120 mL) 100% pomegranate juice

¾ cup (175 mL) canned tomato sauce

1 tbsp (15 mL) unsulfured blackstrap molasses

2 tsp (10 mL) cider vinegar

1½ tsp (7 mL) smoked paprika

1 tsp (5 mL) garlic powder

1 tsp (5 mL) onion powder

¼ tsp (1 mL) salt

¼ tsp (1 mL) freshly ground black pepper

1. In a small bowl, whisk together the pomegranate juice, tomato sauce, molasses, vinegar, paprika, garlic powder, onion powder, salt and pepper.

2. Use immediately or store in a sealable container in the refrigerator for up to 1 week.

SERVING SIZE: 2 tbsp (30 mL)

TOBY'S TIP: Use this barbecue sauce for the Hawaiian Chicken Pizza (page 143) or as a dip for rotisserie chicken.

TZATZIKI

This tangy yogurt-based sauce is typically served in Greek and Turkish cuisines. It can be used as a dip for vegetables or pita, a dressing for salads or a sauce for rotisserie chicken. The trick to making *the best* tzatziki is to make sure to drain the excess liquid from the cucumbers — otherwise, you'll end up with a less than flavorful watery sauce.

1 English (hothouse) cucumber, unpeeled and shredded

¾ cup (175 mL) plain Greek yogurt

¼ cup (60 mL) sour cream

1 clove garlic, minced

2 tbsp (30 mL) chopped fresh dill

1 tsp (5 mL) freshly squeezed lemon juice

¼ tsp (1 mL) salt

⅛ tsp (0.5 mL) freshly ground black pepper

1. Place the shredded cucumber in a colander and set over a large bowl. Using clean hands, squeeze out excess liquid from the cucumber. Discard the liquid from the large bowl.

2. In a medium bowl, add the cucumber, yogurt, sour cream, garlic, dill, lemon juice, salt and black pepper. Cover and refrigerate for 20 minutes to allow the flavors to combine.

3. Use immediately or store in a sealable container in the refrigerator for up to 3 days.

SERVING SIZE: ¼ cup (60 mL)

> **TOBY'S TIPS:** Lighten up this sauce by using nonfat plain Greek yogurt and reduced-fat sour cream.
>
> •
>
> English cucumbers, also known as hothouse cucumbers, do not have large seeds, making them perfect for salads, dips and sauces like this one.

SPICY PEANUT SAUCE

The spiciness in this sauce comes from Thai chile sauce, which you may know as Sriracha sauce (pronounced SIR-rotch-ah). It's made from chile peppers, garlic, sugar, salt and vinegar, which provide a perfect balance of hot, spicy, sweet and tangy flavors. I recommend keeping a bottle on hand at all times because once you give it a try, it's tough *not* to become addicted!

⅓ cup (75 mL) water	1 tsp (5 mL) fish sauce (nam pla)
¼ cup (60 mL) natural creamy peanut butter	1 tsp (5 mL) Thai chile sauce (such as Sriracha)
1 tbsp (15 mL) freshly squeezed lime juice	2 cloves garlic, crushed

1. In a small mixing bowl, whisk together the water, peanut butter, lime juice, fish sauce, Thai chile sauce and garlic. Use immediately or refrigerate in a sealable container for up to 1 week.

SERVING SIZE: 2 tbsp (30 mL)

TOBY'S TIP: Use this sauce as a dip for your rotisserie chicken or with Peanut Chicken and Quinoa Bowls with Broccoli (page 129).

HUMMUS

During my childhood, I spent many summers living in a rented apartment in Israel, where my mother was born. During every meal, hummus was served. As an adult, I still enjoy hummus with my eggs and salads or as a dip for vegetables and chicken. Try pairing this homemade hummus with Mediterranean Orzo and Chicken (page 127), Chicken, Kale and White Bean Salad (page 93) or as a dip for your rotisserie chicken.

BLENDER

14- to 19-oz (398 to 540 mL) can reduced-sodium chickpeas

¼ cup (60 mL) tahini

3 tbsp (45 mL) freshly squeezed lemon juice

2 cloves garlic, minced

2 tbsp (30 mL) water

½ tsp (2 mL) ground cumin

½ tsp (2 mL) salt

⅛ tsp (0.5 mL) freshly ground black pepper

2 tbsp (30 mL) extra virgin olive oil

1. Place the chickpeas, tahini, lemon juice, garlic, water, cumin, salt and pepper into a blender and blend until smooth. With the machine running, gradually add the oil and blend until incorporated.

2. Serve immediately or store in a sealable container in the refrigerator for up to 5 days.

SERVING SIZE: ¼ cup (60 mL)

TOBY'S TIP: Get creative with your hummus by adding ¼ cup (60 mL) fresh parsley, ¼ cup (60 mL) roasted red peppers or 1 tsp (5 mL) Thai chile sauce (such as Sriracha).

CHUNKY SALSA

This mild tomato-based salsa comes together in under 15 minutes. Serve it with a variety of dishes, like White Bean and Chicken Chili (page 130), Weeknight Chicken Soft Tacos (page 132) and Huevos Rancheros with Chicken (page 41).

1 lb (500 g) plum (Roma) tomatoes

1 green bell pepper, chopped

½ red onion, chopped

½ jalapeño pepper, seeded and chopped

¼ cup (60 mL) chopped fresh cilantro

2 tbsp (30 mL) freshly squeezed lime juice

2 tbsp (30 mL) extra virgin olive oil

1 clove garlic, minced

½ tsp (2 mL) salt

⅛ tsp (0.5 mL) freshly ground black pepper

1. In a medium bowl, toss together the tomatoes, green pepper, red onion, jalapeño and cilantro.

2. Add the lime juice, oil, garlic, salt and pepper and toss to evenly coat.

3. Serve immediately or store in a sealable container in the refrigerator for up to 5 days.

SERVING SIZE: ¼ cup (60 mL)

TOBY'S TIP: Want a spicier salsa? Leave the seeds and ribs (the white part) of your jalapeño pepper or use more jalapeños.

ACKNOWLEDGMENTS

THERE ARE MANY people I want to thank for making this cookbook possible. To my children, Schoen, Ellena and Micah, thank you for taste testing your way through meals over the past few months that consisted of lots of rotisserie chicken and for hanging in there through my hectic schedule. All three of you have always been so supportive of my career and I love you all very much. Micah, thank you for being the best twelve-year-old recipe tester assistant a mom could ask for. I am hopeful that one day you will be able to create and test recipes on your own. All three of you are truly the forces that drive everything that I do and have taught me what it means to truly love another human. Thank you to my boyfriend, Tom Welxer, who has been the most supportive through the cookbook writing process and also a top-notch taste tester.

A big thank you to Gail Watson, who has been helping me with my cookbooks for many years. I truly appreciate everything you do. Thank you to my assistant, Christiane Camargo, for helping me with anything and everything that needed to get done.

Last but certainly not least, thank you to Sally Ekus and Lisa Ekus from The Lisa Ekus Group, for your guidance, expertise and support through this process. Thank you to Jaimee Constantine and Sara Pokorny from The Lisa Ekus Group for your support and kindness. Many thanks to Robert Dees, from Robert Rose Inc., for believing in me, and to my editor, Kate Bolen, for working hard to bring this fun and exciting project to life.

Library and Archives Canada Cataloguing in Publication
Title: The best rotisserie chicken cookbook : 100 tasty recipes using a store-bought bird /
Toby Amidor.
Other titles: Rotisserie chicken cookbook
Names: Amidor, Toby, author.
Description: Includes index.
Identifiers: Canadiana 20190229314 | ISBN 9780778806585 (softcover)
Subjects: LCSH: Cooking (Chicken) | LCGFT: Cookbooks.
Classification: LCC TX750.5.C45 A45 2020 | DDC 641.6/65—dc23

INDEX

ABOUT THE AUTHOR

TOBY AMIDOR, MS, RD, CDN, FAND, a veteran in the food and nutrition industry with over twenty years of experience, is an award-winning nutrition expert and *Wall Street Journal* best-selling cookbook author who believes that healthy and wholesome food can also be appetizing and delicious.

Toby is the founder of Toby Amidor Nutrition, PC, where she provides nutrition and food safety consulting servings for individuals, restaurants, commodities and food brands. For over ten years she has been the nutrition expert for FoodNetwork.com and founding contributor to its *Healthy Eats* blog. She is a regular contributor to *U.S. News & World Report Eat + Run* blog, Muscle & Fitness online, Shape.com and SparkPeople.com and she has her own "Ask the Expert" column in *Today's Dietitian* magazine. She has been quoted in hundreds of publications like FoxNews.com, Self.com, ReadersDigest.com, Forbes.com, EatingWell.com and many more. Toby has also appeared on television, including *The Dr. Oz Show, Coffee with America*, Fox 5 NY's *Good Day Street Talk* and *San Antonio Live*. For ten years, she has been an adjunct professor at Teachers College, Columbia University and has also been an adjunct at CUNY Hunter College School of Urban Public Health in New York City. Previously, she was a consultant on several television and online shows, including Bobby Deen's *Not My Mama's Meals*.

Toby is the author of several cookbooks, including *The Greek Yogurt Kitchen: More Than 130 Delicious, Healthy Recipes for Every Meal of the Day* (Grand Central Publishing 2014), *The Healthy Meal Prep Cookbook: Easy and Wholesome Meals to Cook, Prep, Grab and Go* (Rockridge Press 2017), *The Easy 5-Ingredient Healthy Cookbook: Simple Recipes to Make Healthy Eating Delicious* (Rockridge Press 2018), *Smart Meal Prep for Beginners: Recipes and Weekly Plans for Healthy, Ready-to-Go Meals* (Rockridge Press 2018) and *The Create-Your-Plate Diabetes Cookbook: A Plate Method Approach to Simple, Complete Meals* (American Diabetes Association 2020). She is also the nutrition consultant for *The Multi-Cooker Baby Food Cookbook: 100 Easy Recipes for Your Slow Cooker, Pressure Cooker, or Multi-Cooker* by Jenna Helwig (Houghton Mifflin Harcourt 2019).

In 2018, Toby was awarded the coveted Media Excellence Award by the Academy of Nutrition and Dietetics. Toby trained as a clinical dietitian at New York University. Through ongoing consulting and faculty positions, she has established herself as one of the top experts in culinary nutrition, food safety and nutrition communications.